WRIGHT FAMILY PERSONAL PROPERTY TAX LISTS

1782-1850

AMHERST COUNTY
VIRGINIA

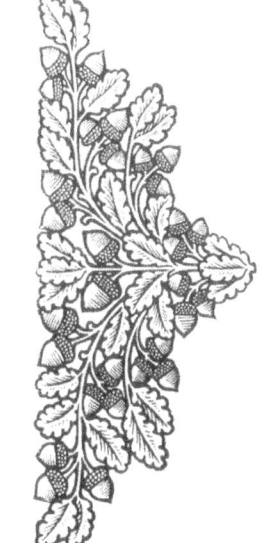

Robert N. Grant

HERITAGE BOOKS
2008

HERITAGE BOOKS
AN IMPRINT OF HERITAGE BOOKS, INC.

Books, CDs, and more—Worldwide

For our listing of thousands of titles see our website

at

www.HeritageBooks.com

Published 2008 by
HERITAGE BOOKS, INC.
Publishing Division
100 Railroad Ave. #104
Westminster, Maryland 21157

Copyright © 2008 Robert N. Grant

All rights reserved. No part of this book may be reproduced or transmitted in any form or by any means, electronic or mechanical, including photocopying, recording or by any information storage and retrieval system without written permission from the author, except for the inclusion of brief quotations in a review.

International Standard Book Numbers
Paperbound: 978-0-7884-4631-3
Clothbound: 978-0-7884-7745-4

Introduction To Appendices: Personal Property Tax List for Amherst County, Virginia

This document is an appendix to a larger work titled Sorting Some Of The Wrights Of Southern Virginia. The work is divided into parts for each family of Wrights that has been researched. Each part is divided into two sections; the first section is text discussing the family and the evidence supporting the relationships and the second section is a descendants chart summarizing the relationships and information known about each individual.

The appendices to the work (of which this document is one) present source records for persons named Wright by county and by type of record with the identification of the person named and their Wright ancestors to the extent known.

The source for the records listed in this appendix is the following:

1) Amherst County, Virginia, Personal Property Tax List, available from The Virginia State Library, 11th & Capitol Streets, Richmond, Virginia 23219-3491.

The identification of a person or their ancestor by year and county indicates their year of death and county of residence at death. For example, "1763 Thomas Wright of Bedford County" indicates that this was the Thomas Wright who died in 1763 in Bedford County. If no state is listed after the county, the state is Virginia; counties in states other than Virginia will have a state listed after the county, as in "1876 William S. Wright of Highland County, Ohio".

A parenthetical after the name indicates an identification of the person when a place of death is not yet known, as in "John Wright (Goochland County Carpenter)". A county in parentheses after the name indicates the county with which that person was most identified when no evidence of the place of death has yet been found, as in "Grief Wright (Bedford County)".

All or portions of the text and descendants charts for each Wright family identified are available from the author:

Robert N. Grant
15 Campo Bello Court   (H) 650-854-0895
Menlo Park, California 94025   (O) 650-614-3800

This is a work in process and I would be most interested in receiving additional information about any of the persons identified in these records in order to correct any errors or expand on the information given.

1927(092807)

1782 PERSONAL PROPERTY TAX LIST

AMHERST COUNTY, VIRGINIA

Appendix: Amherst County, Virginia, 1782 Personal Property Tax List

	Whites	Negroes	Cattle	Horses &c	Wheels for R. Carriages	Billiard Tables	Ordinary License	Identification
Jessee Wright	1		9	2				Jesse Wright (Amherst County)
Killis Wright	1	3	19	3				1825 Achilles Wright of Oldham County, Kentucky
Menos Wright	1		13	2				Parmenos Wright
John Wright	1	1	9	5				John Wright, son of William Wright (Amherst County)
James Wright	1	2	11	5				1839 James Wright of Nelson County, son of William Wright (Amherst County)
William Wright	1	1	12	4				William Wright, Jr., son of William Wright (Amherst County)
Andrew Wright	1		7	2				1816 Andrew Wright of Nelson County, son of William Wright (Amherst County)
Robert Wright	1	1	12	3				1816 Robert Wright of Nelson County, son of William Wright (Amherst County)
Benjamin Wright	1	2	14	6				1799 Benjamin Wright of Amherst County, son of 1767 Francis Wright of Amherst County
Moses Wright	1		6	2				1830 Moses Wright of Amherst County, son of 1799 Benjamin Wright of Amherst County and grandson of 1767 Francis Wright of Amherst County
Isaac Wright	1	9	20	7				1807 Isaac Wright of Amherst County, son of 1767 Francis Wright of Amherst County

Appendix: Amherst County, Virginia, 1782 Personal Property Tax List

	Whites	Negroes	Cattle	Horses &c	Wheels for R. Carriages	Billiard Tables	Ordinary License	Identification
Moses Wright	1		12	2				Moses Wright of Adair County, Kentucky, son of 1767 Francis Wright of Amherst County
Charles Wright				3				

1783 PERSONAL PROPERTY TAX LIST
AMHERST COUNTY, VIRGINIA

Appendix: Amherst County, Virginia, 1783 Personal Property Tax List

	Whites above 21 years	Slaves above 16	Slaves Total	Horses	Cattle	Wheels R.	Ordinary License	Identification
Achillis Wright	1	1	2	3	20			1825 Achilles Wright of Oldham County, Kentucky
Menos Wright	1			2	11			Parmenos Wright
Robert Wright	1			1				1847 Robert Wright of Madison County, Alabama, son of 1776 Augustine Wright of Amherst County
William Wright	1	1	1	3	9			William Wright, Jr., son of William Wright (Amherst County)
Andrew Wright	1		1	3	7			1816 Andrew Wright of Nelson County, son of William Wright (Amherst County)
Robert Wright	1	1	1	5	13			1816 Robert Wright of Nelson County, son of William Wright (Amherst County)
James Wright	1	2	2	6	10			1839 James Wright of Nelson County, son of William Wright (Amherst County)
Benjamin Wright	1	3	3	6	14			1799 Benjamin Wright of Amherst County, son of 1767 Francis Wright of Amherst County
Moses Wright	1			1	5			1830 Moses Wright of Amherst County, son of 1799 Benjamin Wright of Amherst County and grandson of 1767 Francis Wright of Amherst County
John Wright	1	1	1	5	10			John Wright, son of William Wright (Amherst County)
James Wright	1	5	12	6	16			
Thomas Wright	3	4	10	6	22			
Moses Wright	1		2	2	10			Moses Wright of Adair County, Kentucky, son of 1767 Francis Wright of Amherst County

1784 PERSONAL PROPERTY TAX LIST

AMHERST COUNTY, VIRGINIA

Appendix: Amherst County, Virginia, 1784 Personal Property Tax List

	Whites above Twenty one	Slaves above Sixteen	Slaves und. Sixteen	Horses	Head of Cattle	Wheels R. Carriages	Ordin-arys	Stud Horses	Identification
Jessee Wright	1			1	7				Jesse Wright (Amherst County)
Menos Wright	1			2	9				Parmenos Wright
William Wright	1	1		3	9				William Wright, Jr., son of William Wright (Amherst County)
Andrew Wright	1			4	6				1816 Andrew Wright of Nelson County, son of William Wright (Amherst County)
Killis Wright	1	1	2	2	16				1825 Achilles Wright of Oldham County, Kentucky
Augustine Wright Est		2		3	16				Estate of 1776 Augustine Wright of Amherst County
Robert Wright	1	1		7	6				1816 Robert Wright of Nelson County, son of William Wright (Amherst County)
James Wright	1	2		4	14				1839 James Wright of Nelson County, son of William Wright (Amherst County)
John Wright	1	1		4	8				John Wright, son of William Wright (Amherst County)
Moses Wright	1			1	4				1830 Moses Wright of Amherst County, son of 1799 Benjamin Wright of Amherst County and grandson of 1767 Francis Wright of Amherst County
James Wright	1			1					
Benjamin Wright	1	2		6	12				1799 Benjamin Wright of Amherst County, son of 1767 Francis Wright of Amherst County

Appendix: Amherst County, Virginia, 1784 Personal Property Tax List

	Whites above Twenty one	Slaves above Sixteen	Slaves und. Sixteen	Horses	Head of Cattle	Wheels R. Carriages	Ordinarys	Stud Horses	Identification
Isaac Wright	1	4	6	5	16				1807 Isaac Wright of Amherst County, son of 1767 Francis Wright of Amherst County

1785 PERSONAL PROPERTY TAX LIST

AMHERST COUNTY, VIRGINIA

Appendix: Amherst County, Virginia, 1785 Personal Property Tax List

	Whites above 21 years	Whites between 16 & 21	Slaves above 16	Slaves under 16	Head of Horses &c	Head of Cattle	Ordinary Licence	Wheels of Rdg Carriages	Stud Horses pr	Identification
Augustine Wright Estate		2	2		4	16				Estate of 1776 Augustine Wright of Amherst County
Jessee Wright	1				1	8				Jesse Wright (Amherst County)
Archelus Wright	2		1	2	1	13				1825 Achilles Wright of Oldham County, Kentucky
William Wright	1		1		3	7				William Wright, Jr., son of William Wright (Amherst County)
Andrew Wright	1				3	5				1816 Andrew Wright of Nelson County, son of William Wright (Amherst County)
John Wright	1		1		3	2				John Wright, son of William Wright (Amherst County)
Robert Wright (Constable)	1		1		6	8				1816 Robert Wright of Nelson County, son of William Wright (Amherst County)
James Wright	1		2		4	8				1839 James Wright of Nelson County, son of William Wright (Amherst County)

1786 PERSONAL PROPERTY TAX LIST

AMHERST COUNTY, VIRGINIA

Appendix: Amherst County, Virginia, 1786 Personal Property Tax List

	Whites above 21	Whites between 16 & 21	Slaves above Sixteen	Slaves under Sixteen	Horses	Head of Cattle	Ordinary Licenses	Wheels Carriages	Stud Horses Rg the Season	Identification
Jessee Wright	1				2	10				Jesse Wright (Amherst County)
Killis Wright	1	1	1	2	2	13				1825 Achilles Wright of Oldham County, Kentucky
Menos Wright	1	1			2	5				Parmenos Wright
Robert Wright	1		1		5	5				1816 Robert Wright of Nelson County, son of William Wright (Amherst County)
William Wright	1		2		4	9				William Wright, Jr., son of William Wright (Amherst County)
Andrew Wright	1			1	3	5				1816 Andrew Wright of Nelson County, son of William Wright (Amherst County)
James Wright	1	1	2		4	11				1839 James Wright of Nelson County, son of William Wright (Amherst County)
Isaac Wright	2		1	6	9	16				1807 Isaac Wright of Amherst County, son of 1767 Francis Wright of Amherst County
Benjamin Wright	1		2		3	7				1799 Benjamin Wright of Amherst County, son of 1767 Francis Wright of Amherst County
Moses Wright	1				1	4				1830 Moses Wright of Amherst County, son of 1799 Benjamin Wright of Amherst County and grandson of 1767 Francis Wright of Amherst County
Robert Wright	1				1	2				1847 Robert Wright of Madison County, Alabama, son of 1776 Augustine Wright of Amherst County

Appendix: Amherst County, Virginia, 1786 Personal Property Tax List

	Whites above 21	Whites between 16 & 21	Slaves above Sixteen	Slaves under Sixteen	Horses	Head of Cattle	Ordinary Licenses	Wheels Carriages	Stud Horses Rg the Season	Identification
John Wright	1		2		3	5				John Wright, son of William Wright (Amherst County)
William Wright (Clemsons?)	1				2	7				
Mnos Wright	2				2	7				Parmenos Wright [duplicate listing?]

1787 PERSONAL PROPERTY TAX LIST

AMHERST COUNTY, VIRGINIA

Appendix: Amherst County, Virginia, 1787 Personal Property Tax List

Amherst Parish, First District:

Date	Persons names chargeable with the tax	Number of white male Tithables above 21	Number of white males above 16 & under 21	Blacks above 16	Blacks under 16	Horses, mares, colts & mules	Cattle	Carriage Wheels	Ordinary Licenses	Stud Horses
March 29	Samuel Edmunds, Jno. Wright	2		7	1	6	27			
March 29	Benjamin Payne, James Wright		1	0	1	2	0			
March 29	James Wright, Son James	1	1	2	0	6	14			
March 29	William Wright	1	0	2	0	4	8			
May 15	Robert Wright	1	0	1	0	5	7			
May 15	John Wright, Sam'l Fitzgerald	1	1	2	0	4	6			
March 25	Andrew Wright	1	0	1	0	4	6			
May 8	Ackillis Wright, Son Saml.	1	1	3	1	2	14			
May 8	Robert Wright	1	0	1	1	1	4			

Appendix: Amherst County, Virginia, 1787 Personal Property Tax List

Amherst Parish, First District:

Persons names chargeable with the tax [Continued from previous page]	Rate Covering	Identification
Samuel Edmunds, Jno. Wright		John Wright, son of 1776 Augustine Wright of Amherst County
Benjamin Payne, James Wright		
James Wright, Son James		1839 James Wright of Nelson County, son of William Wright (Amherst County) and James Wright, son of 1839 James Wright of Nelson County and grandson of William Wright (Amherst County)
William Wright		William Wright, Jr., son of William Wright (Amherst County)
Robert Wright		1816 Robert Wright of Nelson County, son of William Wright (Amherst County)
John Wright, Sam'l Fitzgerald		John Wright, son of William Wright (Amherst County)
Andrew Wright		1816 Andrew Wright of Amherst County, son of William Wright (Amherst County)
Ackillis Wright, Son Saml.		1825 Achilles Wright of Oldham County, Kentucky and 1824 Samuel Wright of Kentucky, son of 1825 Achilles Wright of Oldham County, Kentucky
Robert Wright		1847 Robert Wright of Madison County, Alabama, son of 1776 Augustine Wright of Amherst County

Appendix: Amherst County, Virginia, 1787 Personal Property Tax List

William Ware District:

Date	Persons chargeable with tax	Whites above 21	Whites between 16 & 21	Blacks over 16	Blacks under 16	Horses	Cattle	Carriage Wheels	Ordinary Licenses	Stud Horses	Rates Covering	Identification
Apl 30	Isaac Wright	Isaac Wright	0	1	6	7	14					1807 Isaac Wright of Amherst County, son of 1767 Francis Wright of Amherst County
Mar 24	Moses Wright	Moses Wright	0	0	0	1	8					Moses Wright of Adair County, Kentucky, son of 1767 Francis Wright of Amherst County
June 5	Benjamin Wright	Benjamin Wright	0	2	0	4	12					1799 Benjamin Wright of Amherst County, son of 1767 Francis Wright of Amherst County
June 5	Mosses Wright	Mosses Wright	0	0	0	1	4					1830 Moses Wright of Amherst County, son of 1799 Benjamin Wright of Amherst County and grandson of 1767 Francis Wright of Amherst County
Apl 2	Jesse Wright	Jesse Wright	0	0	0	1	10					Jesse Wright (Amherst County)

1788 PERSONAL PROPERTY TAX LIST

AMHERST COUNTY, VIRGINIA

Appendix: Amherst County, Virginia, 1788 Personal Property Tax List

List A:

Date	Persons Names Chargd. with Taxes	Number of white Tithables	Slaves Above Sixteen	Slaves between 12 & 16 years	Horses Mules &c	Carriage Wheels	Ordinary License	Stud Horses	at the rate of one Mare the Season	Identification
March 19	James Wright Sr Son James	2	2		6					1839 James Wright of Nelson County, son of William Wright (Amherst County) and James Wright, son of 1839 James Wright of Nelson County and grandson of William Wright (Amherst County)
	Robert Wright	1	1		6					1816 Robert Wright of Nelson County, son of William Wright (Amherst County)
	William Wright Jr.	1			3					William Wright, Jr., son of William Wright (Amherst County)
April 2d	John Wright	1	2		5					John Wright, son of William Wright (Amherst County)
April 2d	Andrew Wright	1	1		3					1816 Andrew Wright of Nelson County, son of William Wright (Amherst County)
April 7th	Jessee Wright	1			1					Jesse Wright (Amherst County)
	Killis Wright Son Samuel	2	3		2					1825 Achilles Wright of Oldham County, Kentucky and 1824 Samuel Wright of Kentucky, son of 1825 Achilles Wright of Oldham County, Kentucky
May 1	Robert Wright Tye river	1	2		1					1847 Robert Wright of Madison County, Alabama, son of 1776 Augustine Wright of Amherst County

Appendix: Amherst County, Virginia, 1788 Personal Property Tax List

List A:

Date	Persons Names Chargd. with Taxes	Number of white Tith- ables	Slaves Above Sixteen	Slaves between 12 & 16 years	Horses Mules &c	Carriage Wheels	Ordinary License	Stud Horses	at the rate of one Mare the Season	Identification
April 25	William Wright Sr Tax free		1							William Wright (Amherst County)

Appendix: Amherst County, Virginia, 1788 Personal Property Tax List

List B:

Date Receiving List	Persons Chargeable with Tax	Tithes	Slaves	Horses	C Wheels	Ordy Licenses	Identification
April 19	Moses Wright	1	0	1			Moses Wright of Adair County, Kentucky, son of 1767 Francis Wright of Amherst County
Aug 1	Isaac Wright	2	2	4			1807 Isaac Wright of Amherst County, son of 1767 Francis Wright of Amherst County
	Benjamin Wright	[unreadable]					1799 Benjamin Wright of Amherst County, son of 1767 Francis Wright of Amherst County
	Moses Wright Junr	[unreadable]					1830 Moses Wright of Amherst County, son of 1799 Benjamin Wright of Amherst County and grandson of 1767 Francis Wright of Amherst County

1789 PERSONAL PROPERTY TAX LIST

AMHERST COUNTY, VIRGINIA

Appendix: Amherst County, Virginia, 1789 Personal Property Tax List

List A:

	Persons Names Charged With Taxes	Number of White Tithables	Slaves over 16 years	Horses Slaves between 12 & 16	Mares Colts & Mules	Carriage Wheels	Ordinary License	Stud Horses	at the Rates of one mare the Season	Identification
March 30th	Andrew Wright	1	1		5					1816 Andrew Wright of Nelson County, son of William Wright (Amherst County)
2d April	James Wright Son Isaac	2	2		6					1839 James Wright of Nelson County, son of William Wright (Amherst County) and Isaac Wright, son of 1839 James Wright of Nelson County and grandson of William Wright (Amherst County)
4th	Robert Wright	1	1		5					1816 Robert Wright of Nelson County, son of William Wright (Amherst County)
6th	William Wright Jun.	1			3					William Wright, Jr., son of William Wright (Amherst County)
8th April	Benjamin Wright Son Jesse	2	2		5					1799 Benjamin Wright of Amherst County, son of 1767 Francis Wright of Amherst County and 1850 Jesse Wright of Nelson County, son of 1799 Benjamin Wright of Amherst County and grandson of 1767 Francis Wright of Amherst County
7th	Killis Wright	1	2	1	3					1825 Achilles Wright of Oldham County, Kentucky
7th	William Wright Senr Tax free		1							William Wright (Amherst County)
11 Jun	Menus Wright	2	1		1					Parmenos Wright

Appendix: Amherst County, Virginia, 1789 Personal Property Tax List

List A:

	Persons Names Charged With Taxes	Number of White Tithables	Slaves over 16 years	Horses Slaves between 12 & 16	Mares Colts & Mules	Carriage Wheels	Ordinary License	Stud Horses	at the Rates of one mare the Season	Identification
July 6	Robert Wright	1	2		2					1847 Robert Wright of Madison County, Alabama, son of 1776 Augustine Wright of Amherst County
Augt. 4	Jessee Wright	1			2					Jesse Wright (Amherst County)

Appendix: Amherst County, Virginia, 1789 Personal Property Tax List

List B:

Date	Persons Charged with Tax	White Tithes	Black Tithes	Blacks between 12 & 16	Horses	C. Wheels	Setts of Billard Tables	No. Ords	Rate Cvrg.	Identification
May 15	Moses Wright Jr	1			1					1830 Moses Wright of Amherst County, son of 1799 Benjamin Wright of Amherst County and grandson of 1767 Francis Wright of Amherst County
July 29	Isaac Wright	2	1		5					1807 Isaac Wright of Amherst County, son of 1767 Francis Wright of Amherst County

1927(102507)

1790 PERSONAL PROPERTY TAX LIST

AMHERST COUNTY, VIRGINIA

Appendix: Amherst County, Virginia, 1790 Personal Property Tax List

List A:

	Persons Names Charged With Taxes	Numb. of Whites	Slaves over 16 years	Slaves between 12 & 16	Horses & Mules	Carriage Wheels	Ordinary License	Stud Horses	at the rate of 1 mare the Season	Identification
March 15	Menus Wright Son Thomas	2			1					Parmenos Wright and Thomas Wright, son of Parmenos Wright
March 29	William Wright Jr.	1		2	3					William Wright, Jr., son of William Wright (Amherst County)
	James Wright Son Isaac	2	2		5					1839 James Wright of Nelson County, son of William Wright (Amherst County) and Isaac Wright, son of 1839 James Wright of Nelson County and grandson of William Wright (Amherst County)
	Andrew Wright	1	1		4					1816 Andrew Wright of Nelson County, son of William Wright (Amherst County)
Apl. 1	John Wright	1			1					John Wright, son of William Wright (Amherst County
	Jesse Wright	1			2					Jesse Wright (Amherst County)
	Robert Wright Tye river	1	1	1	2					1847 Robert Wright of Madison County, Alabama, son of 1776 Augustine Wright of Amherst County

Appendix: Amherst County, Virginia, 1790 Personal Property Tax List

List A:

	Persons Names Charged With Taxes	Numb. of Whites	Slaves over 16 years	Slaves between 12 & 16	Horses & Mules	Carriage Wheels	Ordinary License	Stud Horses	at the rate of 1 mare the Season	Identification
Apl 10	Robert Wright, Son Robert	2	1		4					1816 Robert Wright of Nelson County, son of William Wright (Amherst County) and Robert Wright, son of 1816 Robert Wright of Nelson County and grandson of William Wright (Amherst County)
June 7	Killis Wright	1	3	1	3					1825 Achilles Wright of Oldham County, Kentucky

31.

Appendix: Amherst County, Virginia, 1790 Personal Property Tax List

Lexington Parish:

Persons Names	White Tithes	Black Tithes	Black between 12 & 16	Horses	Identification
Isaac Wright	2	0	1	3	1807 Isaac Wright of Amherst County, son of 1767 Francis Wright of Amherst County
Moses Wright	1	0	0	1	1830 Moses Wright of Amherst County, son of 1799 Benjamin Wright of Amherst County and grandson of 1767 Francis Wright of Amherst County

1791 PERSONAL PROPERTY TAX LIST
AMHERST COUNTY, VIRGINIA

Appendix: Amherst County, Virginia, 1791 Personal Property Tax List

List A:

	Persons Names Charged with Taxes	Numbr. of Whites	Slaves over 16 years	Slaves between 12 & 16	Horses &c	Carriage Wheels	ordinary License	Stud Horses	at the rate of 1 mare the Season	Identification
March 21	Andrew Wright	1			4					1816 Andrew Wright of Nelson County, son of William Wright (Amherst County)
March 21	William Wright (Tyriver)	1			1					William Wright, son of 1776 Augustine Wright of Amherst County
March 21	Robert Wright, Son Robert	2	1		4					1816 Robert Wright of Nelson County, son of William Wright (Amherst County) and Robert Wright, son of 1816 Robert Wright of Nelson County and grandson of William Wright (Amherst County)
May 2	Jesse Wright	1			3					Jesse Wright (Amherst County)
May 2	Menus Wright	1			2					Parmenos Wright
May 2	William Wright	1	1	1	3					William Wright, Jr., son of William Wright (Amherst County)
May 13	James Wright, Sons James & Isaac	3	2		7					1839 James Wright of Nelson County, son of William Wright (Amherst County) and James Wright, son of 1839 James Wright of Nelson County and grandson of William Wright (Amherst County) and Isaac Wright, son of 1839 James Wright of Nelson County and grandson of William Wright (Amherst County)

Appendix: Amherst County, Virginia, 1791 Personal Property Tax List

List A:

	Persons Names Charged with Taxes	Numbr. of Whites	Slaves over 16 years	Slaves between 12 & 16	Horses &c	Carriage Wheels	ordinary License	Stud Horses	at the rate of 1 mare the Season	Identification
June 17	Killis Wright, Son James	2	3	1	3					1825 Achilles Wright of Oldham County, Kentucky and James Wright, son of 1825 Achilles Wright of Oldham County, Kentucky
June 22	Benjamin Wright, Son Jesse	2	2		3					1799 Benjamin Wright of Amherst County, son of 1767 Francis Wright of Amherst County and 1850 Jesse Wright of Nelson County, son of 1799 Benjamin Wright of Amherst County and grandson of 1767 Francis Wright of Amherst County

Appendix: Amherst County, Virginia, 1791 Personal Property Tax List

Lexington Parish:

Date	Persons Names	White Tithes	Slave Tithes	Slaves between 12 & 16 years	Horses Mares &c	No Carriage Wheels	Ordinary Licences	Stud Horses	Rate they cover one mare pr season	Identification
May 2	Moses Wright		1			1				1830 Moses Wright of Amherst County, son of 1799 Benjamin Wright of Amherst County and grandson of 1767 Francis Wright of Amherst County
March 13	Samuel Wright		1							Samuel Wright, son of 1825 Achilles Wright of Oldham County, Kentucky
	Isaac Wright		2	2	1	3				1807 Isaac Wright of Amherst County, son of 1767 Francis Wright of Amherst County

1792 PERSONAL PROPERTY TAX LIST

AMHERST COUNTY, VIRGINIA

Appendix: Amherst County, Virginia, 1792 Personal Property Tax List

List A:

Date	Name	Number of Whites	Slaves over 16	Slaves between 12 & 16	Horses &c	Carriage Wheels	Ordinary License	Stud Horses	At the rate of 1 mare the Season	Identification
April 7	Andrew Wright	1			4			1 @	10/	1816 Andrew Wright of Nelson County, son of William Wright (Amherst County)
April 7	William Wright	1	1	1	4					William Wright, Jr., son of William Wright (Amherst County)
May 4	Jesse Wright	1			3					Jesse Wright (Amherst County)
May 10	Robert Wright (Tyriver)	1	1	1	2					1847 Robert Wright of Madison County, Alabama, son of 1776 Augustine Wright of Amherst County
May 17	Benjamain Wright, Son Jesse	2	2		2					1799 Benjamin Wright of Amherst County, son of 1767 Francis Wright of Amherst County and 1850 Jesse Wright of Nelson County, son of 1799 Benjamin Wright of Amherst County and grandson of 1767 Francis Wright of Amherst County
May 19	Robert Wright, Sons Robert & John	3	1		11					1816 Robert Wright of Nelson County, son of William Wright (Amherst County) and Robert Wright, son of 1816 Robert Wright of Nelson County and grandson of William Wright (Amherst County) and John Wright, son of 1816 Robert Wright of Nelson County and grandson of William Wright (Amherst County)

Appendix: Amherst County, Virginia, 1792 Personal Property Tax List

List A:

		Number of Whites	Slaves over 16	Slaves between 12 & 16	Horses &c	Carriage Wheels	Ordinary License	Stud Horses	At the rate of 1 mare the Season	Identification
June 13	James Wright, Son Isaac	2	2		7					1839 James Wright of Nelson County, son of William Wright (Amherst County) and Isaac Wright, son of 1839 James Wright of Nelson County and grandson of William Wright (Amherst County)
June 26	Killis Wright, Son, James	2	3	1	3					1825 Achilles Wright of Oldham County, Kentucky and James Wright, son of 1825 Achilles Wright of Oldham County, Kentucky
June 26	Menus Wright	1			2					Parmenos Wright

Appendix: Amherst County, Virginia, 1792 Personal Property Tax List

List A:

		Number of Whites	Slaves over 16	Slaves between 12 & 16	Horses &c	Carriage Wheels	Ordinary License	Stud Horses	At the rate of 1 mare the Season	Identification
June 26	Augustine Wright	1								1838 Augustine Wright of Nelson County, son of 1776 Augustine Wright of Amherst County
June 26	David Wright	1			1					
	William Wright (Tyriver)	1			1					William Wright, son of 1776 Augustine Wright of Amherst County

Appendix: Amherst County, Virginia, 1792 Personal Property Tax List

Lexington District:

Date	Persons Names	White Tithes	Negro Tithes	Negroes between 12 & 16	Horses	Identification
	Isaac Wright	-	-	-	-	1807 Isaac Wright of Amherst County, son of 1767 Francis Wright of Amherst County

[Possibly incomplete, partly unreadable]

1793 PERSONAL PROPERTY TAX LIST

AMHERST COUNTY, VIRGINIA

Appendix: Amherst County, Virginia, 1793 Personal Property Tax List

List A:

	Persons Names Charged With Taxes	Number of Whites	Slaves over 16	Slaves between 12 & 16	Horses &c	Carriage Wheels	Ordinary License	Stud Horses	at the rate of 1 mare the Season	Identification
March 13	Menus Wright	1			3					Parmenos Wright
March 13	Killis Wright	1	3	1	4					1825 Achilles Wright of Oldham County, Kentucky
March 18	Jesse Wright	1			3					Jesse Wright (Amherst County)
Apr 12	Robert Wright (Tyriver)	1	2	1	2					1847 Robert Wright of Madison County, Alabama, son of 1776 Augustine Wright of Amherst County
Apl 16	James Wright, Sons Isaac & John	3	2		6					1839 James Wright of Nelson County, son of William Wright (Amherst County) and Isaac Wright, son of 1839 James Wright of Nelson County and grandson of William Wright (Amherst County) and John Wright, son of 1839 James Wright of Nelson County and grandson of William Wright (Amherst County)
Apl 25	Benjamin Wright, Son Jesse	2	2		2					1799 Benjamin Wright of Amherst County, son of 1767 Francis Wright of Amherst County and 1850 Jesse Wright of Nelson County, son of 1799 Benjamin Wright of Amherst County and grandson of 1767 Francis Wright of Amherst County

Appendix: Amherst County, Virginia, 1793 Personal Property Tax List

List A:

	Persons Names Charged With Taxes	Number of Whites	Slaves over 16	Slaves between 12 & 16	Horses &c	Carriage Wheels	Ordinary License	Stud Horses at the rate of 1 mare the Season	Identification
May 20	Andrew Wright	1	1	2	2				1816 Andrew Wright of Nelson County, son of William Wright (Amherst County)
May 23	Robert Wright, Son Robert	2	1		4				1816 Robert Wright of Nelson County, son of William Wright (Amherst County) and Robert Wright, son of 1816 Robert Wright of Nelson County and grandson of William Wright (Amherst County)
June 17	John Wright (Tyriver)	1		1	4				John Wright, son of 1776 Augustine Wright of Amherst County
June 17	William Wright	1	3	0	4				William Wright, Jr., son of William Wright (Amherst County)

Appendix: Amherst County, Virginia, 1793 Personal Property Tax List

Lexington Parrish District:

Dates	Persons Names	White Tithe	Negro Tithes	Negroes between 12 & 16	Horses	Identification
Apl 19	Isaac Wright	2		1	5	1807 Isaac Wright of Amherst County, son of 1767 Francis Wright of Amherst County

1794 PERSONAL PROPERTY TAX LIST

AMHERST COUNTY, VIRGINIA

Appendix: Amherst County, Virginia, 1794 Personal Property Tax List

Amherst Parish:

	Persons Names Charged with Taxes	Whites	Slaves over 16	between 12 & 16	Horses &c	Carriage Wheels	Ordinary License	Stud horses	their rates	Identification
March 7	Andrew Wright	2	1		3			1	10/	1816 Andrew Wright of Nelson County, son of William Wright (Amherst County)
March 7	Jesse Wright	2			3					Jesse Wright (Amherst County)
March 18	John Wright	1	2	1	3					John Wright, son of 1776 Augustine Wright of Amherst County
March 19	Robert Wright (Senr)	2	2		3					1816 Robert Wright of Nelson County, son of William Wright (Amherst County)
Apl 11	David Wright	1			2					
Apl 22	Parmenas Wright	1			2					Parmenos Wright
Apl 26	James Wright & Sons Isaac & John	3	2		7					1839 James Wright of Nelson County, son of William Wright (Amherst County) and Isaac Wright, son of 1839 James Wright of Nelson County and grandson of William Wright (Amherst County) and John Wright, son of 1839 James Wright of Nelson County and grandson of William Wright (Amherst County)
Apl 26	William Wright	1	2		4					William Wright, Jr., son of William Wright (Amherst County)
May 10	George Wright	1			1					George Wright, son of 1825 Achilles Wright of Oldham County, Kentucky
May 10	Killess Wright	1	4		4					1825 Achilles Wright of Oldham County, Kentucky

Appendix: Amherst County, Virginia, 1794 Personal Property Tax List

Amherst Parish:

	Persons Names Charged with Taxes	Whites	Slaves over 16	Slaves between 12 & 16	Horses &c	Carriage Wheels	Ordinary License	Stud horses	their rates	Identification
May 19	Robert Wright (Tye river)	1	3		4					1847 Robert Wright of Madison County, Alabama, son of 1776 Augustine Wright of Amherst County
May 19	William Wright (Tye river)	1			1					William Wright, son of 1776 Augustine Wright of Amherst County
May 22	Benjamin Wright & Son Jesse	2	2		4					1799 Benjamin Wright of Amherst County, son of 1767 Francis Wright of Amherst County and 1850 Jesse Wright of Nelson County, son of 1799 Benjamin Wright of Amherst County and grandson of 1767 Francis Wright of Amherst County

Appendix: Amherst County, Virginia, 1794 Personal Property Tax List

Lexington Parrish:

Dates	Persons Names	White Tithes	Negro Tithes	Negroes between 12 & 16	Horses	Stud Horses Ord Licenses &c	Identification
Apl 21	Isaac Wright	2	1	1	4		1807 Isaac Wright of Amherst County, son of 1767 Francis Wright of Amherst County

1795 PERSONAL PROPERTY TAX LIST

AMHERST COUNTY, VIRGINIA

Appendix: Amherst County, Virginia, 1795 Personal Property Tax List

List A:

	Names	Whites	Neg 16	Neg −16	Horses	Car Wh	O. Lic	Studs	Identification
March 16	Jesse Wright	3			4				Jesse Wright (Amherst County)
March 17	Robert Wright (Tye River	1	3		4				1847 Robert Wright of Madison County, Alabama, son of 1776 Augustine Wright of Amherst County
March 18	John Wright	1	4		3				John Wright, son of 1776 Augustine Wright of Amherst County
Apl 10	James Wright	3	2		7				1839 James Wright of Nelson County, son of William Wright (Amherst County)
Apl 11	William Wright	1	2		4				William Wright, Jr., son of William Wright (Amherst County)
Apl 11	Andrew Wright	2	2		6				1816 Andrew Wright of Nelson County, son of William Wright (Amherst County)
Apl 18	William Wright	1			1				William Wright, son of 1776 Augustine Wright of Amherst County
May 18	James Wright	1			1				Probably 1838 James Wright of Adams County, Mississippi, son of 1816 Robert Wright of Nelson County and grandson of William Wright (Amherst County)
May 18	Robert Wright	2	1		4				1816 Robert Wright of Nelson County, son of William Wright (Amherst County)
May 18	Robert Wright Jr	1			1				Robert Wright, son of 1816 Robert Wright of Nelson County and grandson of William Wright (Amherst County)
May 18	Kelles Wright	1	4		2				1825 Achilles Wright of Oldham County, Kentucky

Appendix: Amherst County, Virginia, 1795 Personal Property Tax List

List A:

	Names	Whites	Neg 16	Neg 16	Horses	Car Wh	O. Lic	Studs	Identification
May 18	George Wright	1							George Wright, son of 1825 Achilles Wright of Oldham County, Kentucky
May 27	Parmenas Wright	1			2				Parmenos Wright
May 27	David Wright	1							
May 27	Thomas Wright	1							Probably Thomas Wright, son of Parmenos Wright
June 8	Benjamin Wright	2	2		2				1799 Benjamin Wright of Amherst County, son of 1767 Francis Wright of Amherst County

Appendix: Amherst County, Virginia, 1795 Personal Property Tax List

Lexington Parish District:

Dates	Persons Names	White Tithes	Negro Tithes	Negroes between 12 & 16	Horses	Stud Horses Ord Licenses &c	Identification
Apl 2	James Wright	1	2		4		
Apl 4	Samuel Wright	1			-		Samuel Wright, son of 1825 Achilles Wright of Oldham County, Kentucky

[Missing Page]

1796 PERSONAL PROPERTY TAX LIST

AMHERST COUNTY, VIRGINIA

Appendix: Amherst County, Virginia, 1796 Personal Property Tax List

List A:

		Whites	Slaves 16	Slaves 12 & 16	Horses	C W	O L	Studs	Rate	Identification
March 28	William Wright	1	2		4					William Wright, Jr., son of William Wright (Amherst County)
March 28	Andrew Wright	1	3		4					1816 Andrew Wright of Nelson County, son of William Wright (Amherst County)
March 31	Benjamin Wright	2	2		2					1799 Benjamin Wright of Amherst County, son of 1767 Francis Wright of Amherst County
Apl 4	John Wright	1	4		2					John Wright, son of 1776 Augustine Wright of Amherst County
Apl 4	Robert Wright	2	1		3					1816 Robert Wright of Nelson County, son of William Wright (Amherst County)
Apl 18	Augustin Wright	1			1					1838 Augustine Wright of Nelson County, son of 1776 Augustine Wright of Amherst County
May 16	Jessee Wright	2			3					Jesse Wright (Amherst County)
May 18	James Wright	2	2		5					1839 James Wright of Nelson County, son of William Wright (Amherst County)
June 20	Minos Wright	1			2					Parmenos Wright
July 1	George Wright	1			1					George Wright, son of 1825 Achilles Wright of Oldham County, Kentucky
July 2	David Wright	1								
July 2	Thomas Wright	1								
July 2	James Wright	1			1					

1927(102507)

56.

Appendix: Amherst County, Virginia, 1796 Personal Property Tax List

Lexington Parrish District:

Dates	Persons Names	White Tithes	Negro Tithes	12 Negroes 21	Horses	Stud Horses Ord Licenses &c	Identification
Apl 9	George Wright	1			2		George Wright, son of 1825 Achilles Wright of Oldham County, Kentucky
Apl 2	Isaac Wright	2	3	1	3		1807 Isaac Wright of Amherst County, son of 1767 Francis Wright of Amherst County
Apl 2	Morriss Wright	1					Morris Wright, son of 1807 Isaac Wright of Amherst County and grandson of 1767 Francis Wright of Amherst County

1797 PERSONAL PROPERTY TAX LIST

AMHERST COUNTY, VIRGINIA

Appendix: Amherst County, Virginia, 1797 Personal Property Tax List

List A:

Month/Day	Persons Names Chargeable	White Tithes	Negroes 16	negroes 16	Horses	C W	O L	Studs	Rates	Identification
March 20	Robert Wright	2	1		2					1816 Robert Wright of Nelson County, son of William Wright (Amherst County)
May 15	Andrew Wright	1	3		4					1816 Andrew Wright of Nelson County, son of William Wright (Amherst County)
May 15	Augustin Wright	1			1					1838 Augustine Wright of Nelson County, son of 1776 Augustine Wright of Amherst County
May 15	John Wright	2	4		3					John Wright, son of 1776 Augustine Wright of Amherst County
May 16	David Wright	1								
May 22	William Wright	1			1					William Wright, son of 1776 Augustine Wright of Amherst County
May 24	William Wright	1	2		4					William Wright, Jr., son of William Wright (Amherst County)
June 1	Jessee Wright jr(?)	1			1					1850 Jesse Wright of Amherst County, son of 1799 Benjamin Wright of Amherst County, and grandson of 1767 Francis Wright of Amherst County
June 19	Jessee Wright	2			3					Jesse Wright (Amherst County)
July 17	James Wright	2	2		5					1839 James Wright of Nelson County, son of William Wright (Amherst County)
July 22	Benjamin Wright	1	2		1					1799 Benjamin Wright of Amherst County, son of 1767 Francis Wright of Amherst County

Appendix: Amherst County, Virginia, 1797 Personal Property Tax List

List A:

Month/Day	Persons Names Chargeable	White Tithes	Negroes 16	negroes 16	Horses	C W	O L	Studs	Rates	Identification
Augt 15	Wiett Wright	1			1					
Augt 15	James Wright	1			1					
Augt 15	Menos Wright	2			2					Parmenos Wright
Augt 15	George Wright	1						6		George Wright, son of 1825 Achilles Wright of Oldham County, Kentucky
Augt 15	Thomas Wright	1								

Appendix: Amherst County, Virginia, 1797 Personal Property Tax List

Lexington Parrish:

Dates	Persons Names	White Tithes	Negro Tithes	12 Negroes 16	Horses	Stud Horses Ord Licenses &c	Identification
Mar 20	Isaac Wright	1	1	1	6		1807 Isaac Wright of Amherst County, son of 1767 Francis Wright of Amherst County
April 1	Mauris Wright	1					Morris Wright, son of 1807 Isaac Wright of Amherst County and grandson of 1767 Francis Wright of Amherst County

1798 PERSONAL PROPERTY TAX LIST

AMHERST COUNTY, VIRGINIA

Appendix: Amherst County, Virginia, 1798 Personal Property Tax List

List A:

	Whites	negroes 16	12 negroes 16	Horses	C	W	O	L	Studs	Rates	Taxes	Identification
George Wright	1											George Wright, son of 1825 Achilles Wright of Oldham County, Kentucky
David Wright	1											
Achilles Wright	1	4		3							1.67	1825 Achilles Wright of Oldham County, Kentucky
William Wright (Tye river)	1			1							.09	William Wright, son of 1776 Augustine Wright of Amherst County
Jessee Wright	2		0	2							.18	Jesse Wright (Amherst County)
Andrew Wright	1	3		5							1.50	1816 Andrew Wright of Nelson County, son of William Wright (Amherst County)
John Wright	1	4		3							1.67	John Wright, son of 1776 Augustine Wright of Amherst County
Robert Wright	2	1		2							.53	1816 Robert Wright of Nelson County, son of William Wright (Amherst County)
James Wright	3	2		5							1.15	1839 James Wright of Nelson County, son of William Wright (Amherst County)
Menos Wright	1	1		2							.53	Parmenos Wright
Jessee Wright	1			1							.09	1850 Jessee Wright of Amherst County, son of 1799 Benjamin Wright of Amherst County, and grandson of 1767 Francis Wright of Amherst County

Appendix: Amherst County, Virginia, 1798 Personal Property Tax List

List A:

	Whites	negroes 16	12 negroes 16	Horses	C	W	O	L	Studs	Rates	Taxes	Identification
William Wright	1	2		5							1.15	William Wright, Jr., son of William Wright (Amherst County)
Benjamin Wright	1	2		2							.88	1799 Benjamin Wright of Amherst County, son of 1767 Francis Wright of Amherst County

Appendix: Amherst County, Virginia, 1798 Personal Property Tax List

Lexington Parrish:

Dates	Persons, Holding Property	White Tithes	Negro Tithes	Negroes Between 12 & 16	Horses	Stud Horses ordinary Licenses Riding carriages	Amt of Tax	Identification
Mar 11	Isaac Wright	1	1	1	3		.97	1807 Isaac Wright of Amherst County, son of 1767 Francis Wright of Amherst County
June 25	Samuel Wright	1			1		.09	Samuel Wright, son of 1825 Achilles Wright of Oldham County, Kentucky
July 10	Mauris Wright	1			1		.09	Morris Wright, son of 1807 Isaac Wright of Amherst County and grandson of 1767 Francis Wright of Amherst County

1799 PERSONAL PROPERTY TAX LIST

AMHERST COUNTY, VIRGINIA

Appendix: Amherst County, Virginia, 1799 Personal Property Tax List

Amherst Parish:

	Whites	negroes 16	12 negroes 16	Horses	O L	Taxes Amt	Identification
Augustin Wright	1	1		1		.56	1838 Augustine Wright of Nelson County, son of 1776 Augustine Wright of Amherst County
Linsey Wright	1						Lindsay Wright, son of Jesse Wright (Amherst County)
Jessee Wright	1			2		.24	Jesse Wright (Amherst County)
David Wright	1			2		.24	
Jessee Wright	1		1	1		.56	1850 Jesse Wright of Nelson County, son of 1799 Benjamin Wright of Amherst County and grandson of 1767 Francis Wright of Amherst County
John Wright	1	4	1	4		2.68	John Wright, son of 1776 Augustine Wright of Amherst County
James Wright	4	2		6		1.60	1839 James Wright of Nelson County, son of William Wright (Amherst County)
Robert Wright	1	1		3		1.24	1816 Robert Wright of Nelson County, son of William Wright (Amherst County)
Andrew Wright	1	3		5		1.92	1816 Andrew Wright of Nelson County, son of William Wright (Amherst County)
William Wright	1	2		4		1.36	William Wright, Jr., son of William Wright (Amherst County)
George Wright	1						George Wright, son of 1825 Achilles Wright of Oldham County, Kentucky
Achilles Wright	1	4		3		2.12	1825 Achilles Wright of Oldham County, Kentucky
William Wright	1			1		.12	William Wright, son of 1776 Augustine Wright of Amherst County
Menos Wright	1	1		2		.68	Parmenos Wright

Appendix: Amherst County, Virginia, 1799 Personal Property Tax List

Amherst Parish:

	Whites	negroes 16	12 negroes 16	Horses	O L	Taxes Amt	Identification
Benjamin Wright	1	2		2		1.12	1799 Benjamin Wright of Amherst County, son of 1767 Francis Wright of Amherst County

Appendix: Amherst County, Virginia, 1799 Personal Property Tax List

Lexington Parrish:

Dates	Persons Names	White Tithes	Negro Tithes	Negroes Between 12 & 16	Horses	Stud Horses ordinary Licenses Riding Carriages	Amount of Tax	Identification
March 14	Morris Wright	1	1		1		.56	Morris Wright, son of 1807 Isaac Wright of Amherst County and grandson of 1767 Francis Wright of Amherst County
March 14	Isaac Wright jr	1			1		.12	Isaac Wright, son of 1807 Isaac Wright of Amherst County and grandson of 1767 Francis Wright of Amherst County
March 18	Samuel Wright	1			1		.12	Samuel Wright, son of 1825 Achilles Wright of Oldham County, Kentucky
July 6	Isaac Wright	1	2		2		1.12	1807 Isaac Wright of Amherst County, son of 1767 Francis Wright of Amherst County

1800 PERSONAL PROPERTY TAX LIST

AMHERST COUNTY, VIRGINIA

Appendix: Amherst County, Virginia, 1800 Personal Property Tax List

List A:

	White tithes	negroes 16	12 negroes 16	Horses &c	O L	Taxes	Identification
David Wright	1			1		.44	
James Wright	1						
John Wright	1	4	1	3		2.56	
William Wright	1			1		.12	William Wright, son of 1776 Augustine Wright of Amherst County
William Wright	1	2		3		1.24	William Wright, Jr., son of William Wright (Amherst County)
Robert Wright	1	1		3		.80	1816 Robert Wright of Nelson County, son of William Wright (Amherst County)
Menos Wright	1			1		.12	Parmenos Wright
Jordan Wright	1	1		1		.56	1804 Jordan Wright of Amherst County, son of Parmenos Wright
Richard Wright	1						1805 Richard Wright of Amherst County, son of Parmenos Wright
Jessee Wright	1			2		.24	Jesse Wright (Amherst County)
Linsey Wright	1						Lindsay Wright, son of Jesse Wright (Amherst County)
Andrew Wright	2	3		6		2.04	1816 Andrew Wright of Nelson County, son of William Wright (Amherst County)
James Wright jr	1			2		.24	James Wright, son of 1839 James Wright of Nelson County and grandson of William Wright (Amherst County)
Jessee Wright jr	1	1		1		.56	1850 Jesse Wright of Amherst County, son of 1799 Benjamin Wright of Amherst County, and grandson of 1767 Francis Wright of Amherst County

Appendix: Amherst County, Virginia, 1800 Personal Property Tax List

List A:

	White tithes	negroes 16	12 negroes 16	Horses &c	O L	Taxes	Identification
Est of Benjamin Wright		2		2		1.12	Estate of 1799 Benjamin Wright of Amherst County, son of 1767 Francis Wright of Amherst County
John Wright	1						
Achilles Wright	1	3		2		1.56	1825 Achilles Wright of Oldham County, Kentucky
James Wright (Son of Robt)	1						1838 James Wright of Adams County, Mississippi, son of 1816 Robert Wright of Nelson County and grandson of William Wright (Amherst County)
Augustin Wright	1	1	0	1		.56	1838 Augustine Wright of Nelson County, son of 1776 Augustine Wright of Amherst County
Thomas Wright	1			1		.12	
James Wright senr						1.60	1839 James Wright of Nelson County, son of William Wright (Amherst County)

1927(102507)

73.

Appendix: Amherst County, Virginia, 1800 Personal Property Tax List

Lexington Parrish:

Dates	Persons Names	W	T		Amt.	Identification
March 31	Isaac Wright	1	2	2	1.12	1807 Isaac Wright of Amherst County, son of 1767 Francis Wright of Amherst County
Apl. 19	Moses Wright	3		2	.24	1830 Moses Wright of Amherst County, son of 1799 Benjamin Wright of Amherst County and grandson of 1767 Francis Wright of Amherst County
May 16	Morris Wright	1		1	.12	Morris Wright, son of 1807 Isaac Wright of Amherst County and grandson of 1767 Francis Wright of Amherst County
June 17	Samuel Wright	1	2	1	1.00	Samuel Wright, son of 1825 Achilles Wright of Oldham County, Kentucky
Aug 19	Isaac Wright jr	1				Isaac Wright, son of 1807 Isaac Wright of Amherst County and grandson of 1767 Francis Wright of Amherst County

1801 PERSONAL PROPERTY TAX LIST

AMHERST COUNTY, VIRGINIA

Appendix: Amherst County, Virginia, 1801 Personal Property Tax List

Amherst Parish:

	White Tithes	negroes 16	12 negroes 16	Horses &c	Studs	Taxes Cents	Identification
Lindsey Wright	1			1		.12	Lindsay Wright, son of Jesse Wright (Amherst County)
Andrew Wright	1	3		5		1.92	1816 Andrew Wright of Nelson County, son of William Wright (Amherst County)
John Wright	1						
Augustin Wright	1			1		.12	1838 Augustine Wright of Nelson County, son of 1776 Augustine Wright of Amherst County
James Wright jr	1			2		.24	
William Wright	1	2		3		1.24	William Wright, Jr., son of William Wright (Amherst County)
James Wright (Son of James)	1			1		.12	James Wright, son of 1839 James Wright of Nelson County and grandson of William Wright (Amherst County)
Menos Wright	1	1		3		.80	Parmenos Wright
Jordan Wright	1	1	1	1		1.00	1804 Jordan Wright of Amherst County, son of Parmenos Wright
Richard Wright	1			1		.12	1805 Richard Wright of Amherst County, son of Parmenos Wright
Thomas Wright	1						
Jessee Wright	1			2		.24	Jesse Wright (Amherst County)
John Wright (Son of James)	1			1		.12	John Wright, son of 1839 James Wright of Nelson County and grandson of William Wright (Amherst County)
Achilles Wright	1	5	1	3		3.00	1825 Achilles Wright of Oldham County, Kentucky

Appendix: Amherst County, Virginia, 1801 Personal Property Tax List

Amherst Parish:

	White Tithes	negroes 16	12 negroes 16	Horses &c	Studs	Taxes Cents	Identification
James Wright Senr	2	3		6		2.04	1839 James Wright of Nelson County, son of William Wright (Amherst County)
Jessee Wright	1	1		1		.56	1850 Jesse Wright of Nelson County, son of 1799 Benjamin Wright of Amherst County and grandson of 1767 Francis Wright of Amherst County
Est Benjamin Wright		2	1	2		1.56	Estate of 1799 Benjamin Wright of Amherst County, son of 1767 Francis Wright of Amherst County

Appendix: Amherst County, Virginia, 1801 Personal Property Tax List

Lexington Parish District:

Dates	Persons Names	White tithes	Negroe tithes	Negroes betw. 12 & 16	horses	Stud horses ordy Licenses & Riding Carriages	Amtt. of Tax	Identification
March 16	Isaac Wright	2	2		2		1.12	1807 Isaac Wright of Amherst County, son of 1767 Francis Wright of Amherst County
March 19	Samuel Wright	1	1		1		.56	Samuel Wright, son of 1825 Achilles Wright of Oldham County, Kentucky
Apl 18	Moses Wright	1			2		.24	1830 Moses Wright of Amherst County, son of 1799 Benjamin Wright of Amherst County and grandson of 1767 Francis Wright of Amherst County
May 8	Morris Wright	1			1		.12	Morris Wright, son of 1807 Isaac Wright of Amherst County and grandson of 1767 Francis Wright of Amherst County
May 8	Isaac Wright jr	1			1		.12	Isaac Wright, son of 1807 Isaac Wright of Amherst County and grandson of 1767 Francis Wright of Amherst County
__ 20	John Wright	1						John W. Wright, son of 1830 Moses Wright of Anmherst County, grandson of 1799 Benjamin Wright of Amherst County, and great grandson of 1767 Francis Wright of Amherst County

1802 PERSONAL PROPERTY TAX LIST

AMHERST COUNTY, VIRGINIA

Appendix: Amherst County, Virginia, 1802 Personal Property Tax List

Amherst Parish:

	Whites	Negroes 16	12 Negroes 16	Horses	C W	Or. L.	Stud Horses	Dollars Cents	Identification
John Wright	1	5		5				2.80	John Wright, son of 1776 Augustine Wright of Amherst County
Robert Wright	1	2		3				1.24	1816 Robert Wright of Nelson County, son of William Wright (Amherst County)
Austuin Wright	1			1				.12	1838 Augustine Wright of Nelson County, son of 1776 Augustine Wright of Amherst County
Jessee Wright	1			2				.24	Jesse Wright, Jr., son of Jesse Wright, Sr. (Amherst County)
Linzey Wright	1			1				.12	Lindsay Wright, son of Jesse Wright (Amherst County)
Achillis Wright	1	3		3				1.68	1825 Achilles Wright of Oldham County, Kentucky
William Wright	1	2		3				1.24	William Wright, Jr., son of William Wright (Amherst County)
John Wright	1	1		1				.56	
James Wright jr	1			1				.12	
James Wright Senr	2	3		5				1.72	1839 James Wright of Nelson County, son of William Wright (Amherst County)
John Wright (Son James)	1			1				.12	John Wright, son of 1839 James Wright of Nelson County and grandson of William Wright (Amherst County)

Appendix: Amherst County, Virginia, 1802 Personal Property Tax List

Amherst Parish:

	Whites	Negroes 16	Negroes 12 16	Horses	Horses C W	Or. L.	Stud Horses	Dollars Cents	Identification
George Wright	1			1				.12	George Wright, son of 1825 Achilles Wright of Oldham County, Kentucky
John Wright	1								
James Wright (son James)	1			1				.12	James Wright, son of 1839 James Wright of Nelson County and grandson of William Wright (Amherst County)
Richard Wright	1			1				.12	1805 Richard Wright of Amherst County, son of Parmenos Wright
Thomas Wright	1								
Jessee Wright Senr	1			1				.12	Jesse Wright (Amherst County)
Andrew Wright	2	3		7				2.16	1816 Andrew Wright of Nelson County, son of William Wright (Amherst County)
Thomas Wright	1								

Appendix: Amherst County, Virginia, 1802 Personal Property Tax List

Lexington Parish:

Persons Names	White tithes	Negroe tithes	Negroes betw. 12 & 16	horses	Stud horses Ordy Licenses and Riding Carriages	Amount of taxes	Identification
Isaac Wright	2	2		3		1.24	1807 Isaac Wright of Amherst County, son of 1767 Francis Wright of Amherst County
Samuel Wright	1	1		1		.56	Samuel Wright, son of 1825 Achilles Wright of Oldham County, Kentucky
Moses Wright	2			2		.24	1830 Moses Wright of Amherst County, son of 1799 Benjamin Wright of Amherst County and grandson of 1767 Francis Wright of Amherst County
Isaac Wright jr	1						Isaac Wright, son of 1807 Isaac Wright of Amherst County and grandson of 1767 Francis Wright of Amherst County
Morriss Wright	1			1		.12	Morris Wright, son of 1807 Isaac Wright of Amherst County and grandson of 1767 Francis Wright of Amherst County
John Wright (son Moses)	1						John W. Wright, son of 1830 Moses Wright of Amherst County, grandson of 1799 Benjamin Wright of Amherst County, and great grandson of 1767 Francis Wright of Amherst County

1803 PERSONAL PROPERTY TAX LIST

AMHERST COUNTY, VIRGINIA

Appendix: Amherst County, Virginia, 1803 Personal Property Tax List

Amherst Parish:

	Whites	Negroes 16	Negroes Between 12 & 16	Horses	Stud Horses	Carriages	Ordinary Licenses	Seins	Dollars Cents	Identification
John Wright (P. River)	1	1		3					.80	John Wright, son of 1776 Augustine Wright of Amherst County
Andrew Wright	1	2	1	10					2.52	1816 Andrew Wright of Nelson County, son of William Wright (Amherst County)
James Wright Snr	3	4	2	8					2.60	1839 James Wright of Nelson County, son of William Wright (Amherst County)
Jessee Wright jr	1			1					.12	Jesse Wright, Jr., son of Jesse Wright, Sr. (Amherst County)
Lindsey Wright	1									Lindsay Wright, son of Jesse Wright (Amherst County)
Jorden Wright	1	1		1					.56	1804 Jordan Wright of Amherst County, son of Parmenos Wright
Landon Wright	1	1		1					.56	
Parmenis Wright	1									Parmenos Wright
John Wright (Son Robert)	1	1		1					.56	John Wright, son of 1816 Robert Wright of Nelson County and grandson of William Wright (Amherst County)
Geo Wright	1									George Wright, son of 1825 Achilles Wright of Oldham County, Kentucky
Achilles Wright	1	4		3					2.12	1825 Achilles Wright of Oldham County, Kentucky

Appendix: Amherst County, Virginia, 1803 Personal Property Tax List

Amherst Parish:

	Whites	Negroes 16	Negroes Between 12 & 16	Horses	Stud Horses	Carriages	Ordinary Licenses	Seins	Dollars Cents	Identification
Ro Wright	1	2		4					1.36	1816 Robert Wright of Nelson County, son of William Wright (Amherst County)
James Wright Senr	3	4	2	8					3.60	1839 James Wright of Nelson County, son of William Wright (Amherst County) [duplicate listing]
Jessee Wright jr	1			1					.12	1850 Jesse Wright of Amherst County, son of 1799 Benjamin Wright of Amherst County, and grandson of 1767 Francis Wright of Amherst County [duplicate listing]
Lindsey Wright	1									Lindsay Wright, son of Jesse Wright (Amherst County) [duplicate listing]
Jorden Wright	1	1		1					.56	1804 Jordan Wright of Amherst County, son of Parmenos Wright [duplicate listing]
Landen Wright	1		1	1					.56	[duplicate listing]
Parmenus Wright	1									Parmenos Wright [duplicate listing]

Appendix: Amherst County, Virginia, 1803 Personal Property Tax List

Lexington Parish District:

Persons Names	White tithes	Negroe tithes	Negroes betw. 12 & 16	Horses	Stud horses ordy Licenses & Ridg Carages	Amt. of Taxes	Identification
Isaac Wright	1	3	1	5		1.92	1807 Isaac Wright of Amherst County, son of 1767 Francis Wright of Amherst County
Benjamin Wright	1			1		.12	Benjamin Wright of Amherst County, son of 1830 Moses Wright of Amherst County, grandson of 1799 Benjamin Wright of Amherst County, and great grandson of 1767 Francis Wright of Amherst County
Isaac Wright Junr	1						Isaac Wright, son of 1807 Isaac Wright of Amherst County and grandson of 1767 Francis Wright of Amherst County
Ellis Wright	1						1860 Ellis Wright of Wayne County, Kentucky, son of 1807 Isaac Wright of Amherst County and grandson of 1767 Francis Wright of Amherst County
Morriss Wright	1			1		.12	Morris Wright, son of 1807 Isaac Wright of Amherst County and grandson of 1767 Francis Wright of Amherst County
Moses Wright	1			3		.36	1830 Moses Wright of Amherst County, son of 1799 Benjamin Wright of Amherst County and grandson of 1767 Francis Wright of Amherst County
Samuel Wright	1	1		1		.56	Samuel Wright, son of 1825 Achilles Wright of Oldham County, Kentucky

1804 PERSONAL PROPERTY TAX LIST

AMHERST COUNTY, VIRGINIA

Appendix: Amherst County, Virginia, 1804 Personal Property Tax List

List A:

Name						Identification
Robert Wright	1	1		4	.92	1816 Robert Wright of Nelson County, son of William Wright (Amherst County)
James Wright	1	1		2	.68	
Andrew Wright	2	1	1	7	1.72	1816 Andrew Wright of Nelson County, son of William Wright (Amherst County)
Geo Wright	1	1				George Wright, son of 1825 Achilles Wright of Oldham County, Kentucky
John Wright	1	3		7	2.06	John Wright, son of 1776 Augustine Wright of Amherst County
William Wright	1	2		5	1.48	William Wright, Jr., son of William Wright (Amherst County)
James Wright	1					
Achilles Wright	1	4		3	2.12	1825 Achilles Wright of Oldham County, Kentucky
Jessee Wright (P River)	1	1		3	.80	1850 Jesse Wright of Nelson County, son of 1799 Benjamin Wright of Amherst County and grandson of 1767 Francis Wright of Amherst County
John Wright (son R)	1	1		1	.56	John Wright, son of 1816 Robert Wright of Nelson County and grandson of William Wright (Amherst County)
James Wright Sr	3	4	2	8	3.60	1839 James Wright of Nelson County, son of William Wright (Amherst County)
Jesse Wright Sr	1					Jesse Wright (Amherst County)

1927(102507)

Appendix: Amherst County, Virginia, 1804 Personal Property Tax List

List A:

			Identification
Jesse Wright jr	1		Jesse Wright, probably son of Jesse Wright (Amherst County)
Lindsey Wright	1		Lindsay Wright, son of Jesse Wright (Amherst County)
Jordan Wright	1	.56	1804 Jordan Wright of Amherst County, son of Parmenos Wright
Landon Wright	1	.56	

1927(102507)

Appendix: Amherst County, Virginia, 1804 Personal Property Tax List

Lexington Parish:

Persons Names	Free Male tithes	Negroe tithes	Negroes betw. 12 & 16	horses	Stud horses ordy license and Riding Carages	Amount of Tax	Identification
Isaac Wright	2	1		6		1.46	1807 Isaac Wright of Amherst County, son of 1767 Francis Wright of Amherst County
Isaac Wright Jur	1			1		.12	Isaac Wright, son of 1807 Isaac Wright of Amherst County and grandson of 1767 Francis Wright of Amherst County
Moses Wright	1			3		.36	1830 Moses Wright of Amherst County, son of 1799 Benjamin Wright of Amherst County and grandson of 1767 Francis Wright of Amherst County
John Wright (son Moses)	1			1		.12	John W. Wright, son of 1830 Moses Wright of Amherst County, grandson of 1799 Benjamin Wright of Amherst County, and great grandson of 1767 Francis Wright of Amherst County
Benjamin Wright	1			2		.24	Benjamin Wright of Amherst County, son of 1830 Moses Wright of Amherst County, grandson of 1799 Benjamin Wright of Amherst County, and great grandson of 1767 Francis Wright of Amherst County
Morriss Wright	1			1		.12	Morris Wright, son of 1807 Isaac Wright of Amherst County and grandson of 1767 Francis Wright of Amherst County
Ellis Wright	1						1860 Ellis Wright of Wayne County, Kentucky, son of 1807 Isaac Wright of Amherst County and grandson of 1767 Francis Wright of Amherst County
John Wright	1			1		.12	

1805 PERSONAL PROPERTY TAX LIST

AMHERST COUNTY, VIRGINIA

Appendix: Amherst County, Virginia, 1805 Personal Property Tax List

List A:

				Identification
Jessee Wright	1	1		1850 Jesse Wright of Amherst County, son of 1799 Benjamin Wright of Amherst County, and grandson of 1767 Francis Wright of Amherst County
Est. Ben Wright	1	3		Estate of 1799 Benjamin Wright of Amherst County, son of 1767 Francis Wright of Amherst County
Robt. Wright	1	1	1	1816 Robert Wright of Nelson County, son of William Wright (Amherst County)
John Wright (SR)	1	1		John Wright, son of 1816 Robert Wright of Nelson County and grandson of William Wright (Amherst County)
Austin Wright	1	1		1838 Augustine Wright of Nelson County, son of 1776 Augustine Wright of Amherst County
Parmenus Wright	1			Parmenos Wright
William Wright	1	2		William Wright, Jr., son of William Wright (Amherst County)
Andrew Wright	1	2	2	1816 Andrew Wright of Nelson County, son of William Wright (Amherst County)
Benjamin Wright	1			Benjamin Wright of Amherst County, son of 1830 Moses Wright of Amherst County, grandson of 1799 Benjamin Wright of Amherst County, and great grandson of 1767 Francis Wright of Amherst County
Jessee Wright	1			Jesse Wright (Amherst County)
Lindsey Wright	1			Lindsay Wright, son of Jesse Wright (Amherst County)
Achilus Wright	1	4	3	1825 Achilles Wright of Oldham County, Kentucky

Appendix: Amherst County, Virginia, 1805 Personal Property Tax List

List A:

				Identification
James Wright (son J)	1		1	James Wright, son of 1839 James Wright of Nelson County and grandson of William Wright (Amherst County)
George Wright	1			George Wright, son of 1825 Achilles Wright of Oldham County, Kentucky
John Wright (SR)	1	1	1	
John Wright	1	3	7	John Wright, son of 1776 Augustine Wright of Amherst County
James Wright	3	4	2	8	1839 James Wright of Nelson County, son of William Wright (Amherst County)
Landon Wright	1		1	

1927(102507)

Appendix: Amherst County, Virginia, 1805 Personal Property Tax List

Lexington Parish:

Persons Names	Free Tithes	Negro Tithes	Negroes betw. 12 & 16	horses	Stud Horses Riding Carriages & Ordinary Licenses	Amount of Tax	Identification
Bennett Wright	1						1876 Bennett Crawford Wright of Missouri, son of 1807 Isaac Wright of Amherst County and grandson of 1767 Francis Wright of Amherst County
Isaac Wright Jur	1						Isaac Wright, son of 1807 Isaac Wright of Amherst County and grandson of 1767 Francis Wright of Amherst County
Isaac Wright Sen.	2	2		6		1.60	1807 Isaac Wright of Amherst County, son of 1767 Francis Wright of Amherst County
Moses Wright	1			3		.36	1830 Moses Wright of Amherst County, son of 1799 Benjamin Wright of Amherst County and grandson of 1767 Francis Wright of Amherst County
Ellis Wright	1						1860 Ellis Wright of Wayne County, Kentucky, son of 1807 Isaac Wright of Amherst County and grandson of 1767 Francis Wright of Amherst County
Morriss Wright	1	1		1		.13	Morris Wright, son of 1807 Isaac Wright of Amherst County and grandson of 1767 Francis Wright of Amherst County
John Wright (SM)	1			1		.12	John W. Wright, son of 1830 Moses Wright of Amherst County, grandson of 1799 Benjamin Wright of Amherst County, and great grandson of 1767 Francis Wright of Amherst County

1806 PERSONAL PROPERTY TAX LIST

AMHERST COUNTY, VIRGINIA

Appendix: Amherst County, Virginia, 1806 Personal Property Tax List

List A:

	Whites Over 16	Blacks Over 16	Blacks between 12 & 16	Horses &c	Stud horses	Rates of coverg a mare	two wheeled Carriages	Phaetons & stage waggons	Other four wheeled Carriages	Seins	Identification
Robert Wright	1	1	1	4							1816 Robert Wright of Nelson County, son of William Wright (Amherst County)
John Wright	1	1		1							
Jas. Wright jr	1			2							
Achillis Wright	2	4		3							1825 Achilles Wright of Oldham County, Kentucky
John Wright	1	2		3							John Wright, son of 1776 Augustine Wright of Amherst County
Jesse Wright jr	1			2							
Minous Wright	4	1		3							Parmenos Wright
George Wright	1			1							George Wright, son of 1825 Achilles Wright of Oldham County, Kentucky
Jesse Wright	1										
Andrew Wright	1	3	1	6							1816 Andrew Wright of Nelson County, son of William Wright (Amherst County)
Jas Wright Senr	1	2	2	4							1839 James Wright of Nelson County, son of William Wright (Amherst County)

1927(102507)

Appendix: Amherst County, Virginia, 1806 Personal Property Tax List

List A:

	Whites Over 16	Blacks Over 16	Blacks between 12 & 16	Horses &c	Stud horses	Rates of coverg a mare	two wheeled Carriages	Phaetons & stage waggons	Other four wheeled Carriges	Seins	Identification
Allxr. Wright	1			2							1861 Alexander Wright of Holt County, Missouri, son of 1839 James Wright of Nelson County and grandson of William Wright (Amherst County)
Jno. Wright (Son Robt)	1	1									John Wright, son of 1816 Robert Wright of Nelson County and grandson of William Wright (Amherst County)
Benjn Wright	1										Benjamin Wright of Amherst County, son of 1830 Moses Wright of Amherst County, grandson of 1799 Benjamin Wright of Amherst County, and great grandson of 1767 Francis Wright of Amherst County
Wm Wright	1	2		5							William Wright, Jr., son of William Wright (Amherst County)
Estate Benj Wright		3		1							Estate of 1799 Benjamin Wright of Amherst County, son of 1767 Francis Wright of Amherst County
Jesse Wright (PR)	1	2		3							1850 Jesse Wright of Nelson County, son of 1799 Benjamin Wright of Amherst County and grandson of 1767 Francis Wright of Amherst County

Appendix: Amherst County, Virginia, 1806 Personal Property Tax List

List A:

	Whites Over 16	Blacks Over 16	Blacks between 12 & 16	Horses &c	Stud horses	Rates of coverg a mare	two wheeled Carriages	Phaetons & stage waggons	Other four wheeled Carriges	Seins	Identification
Austin Wright	1	1									1838 Augustine Wright of Nelson County, son of 1776 Augustine Wright of Amherst County

Appendix: Amherst County, Virginia, 1806 Personal Property Tax List

Lexington Parish:

Persons Names	Free Tithes	Negro Tithes	Negr betw. 12 & 16	Horses	Riding Cariages and Stud Horses	Amount of Tax	Identification
Isaac Wright	2	3		5			1807 Isaac Wright of Amherst County, son of 1767 Francis Wright of Amherst County
Isaac Wright Jur	1						Isaac Wright, son of 1807 Isaac Wright of Amherst County and grandson of 1767 Francis Wright of Amherst County
Morriss Wright	1			2			Morris Wright, son of 1807 Isaac Wright of Amherst County and grandson of 1767 Francis Wright of Amherst County
Moses Wright	1		1	2			1830 Moses Wright of Amherst County, son of 1799 Benjamin Wright of Amherst County and grandson of 1767 Francis Wright of Amherst County
John Wright SM	1			1			John W. Wright, son of 1830 Moses Wright of Amherst County, grandson of 1799 Benjamin Wright of Amherst County, and great grandson of 1767 Francis Wright of Amherst County

1807 PERSONAL PROPERTY TAX LIST

AMHERST COUNTY, VIRGINIA

Appendix: Amherst County, Virginia, 1807 Personal Property Tax List

Amherst Parish:

	White	Black over 16 Years	Blacks between 12 & 16	Horses	Stud Horses riding Cariages & Seins	Identification
John Wright (Nab(?))	2	1		5		John Wright, son of 1776 Augustine Wright of Amherst County
Robt Wright	1	1	1	6		1816 Robert Wright of Nelson County, son of William Wright (Amherst County)
John Wright (Son Rot)	1	1				John Wright, son of 1816 Robert Wright of Nelson County and grandson of William Wright (Amherst County)
James Wright Senr	1	3		5		1839 James Wright of Nelson County, son of William Wright (Amherst County)
Alexdr Wright	1			2		1861 Alexander Wright of Holt County, Missouri, son of 1839 James Wright of Nelson County and grandson of William Wright (Amherst County)
Andrew Wright	1	3	1	8		1816 Andrew Wright of Nelson County, son of William Wright (Amherst County)
Archillis Wright	2	4		3		1825 Achilles Wright of Oldham County, Kentucky
John Wright (son Jas)	1	1		1		John Wright, son of 1839 James Wright of Nelson County and grandson of William Wright (Amherst County)
James Wright (son Jas)	1			1		James Wright, son of 1839 James Wright of Nelson County and grandson of William Wright (Amherst County)
Minous Wright	1			1		Parmenos Wright
Revrd Wm. Wright				1		1851 William Wright (Amherst County), probably son of William Wright, Jr., and grandson of William Wright (Amherst County)
Wm Wright	1	3		6		William Wright, Jr., son of William Wright (Amherst County)

Appendix: Amherst County, Virginia, 1807 Personal Property Tax List

Amherst Parish:

	White	Black over 16 Years	Blacks between 12 & 16	Horses	Stud Horses riding Cariages & Seins	Identification
Benjn Wright	1					1861 Benjamin Wright of Nelson County, son of 1816 Andrew Wright of Nelson County and grandson of William Wright (Amherst County)
Austin Wright	1	1				1838 Augustine Wright of Nelson County, son of 1776 Augustine Wright of Amherst County
James Wright qt	1			2		
Estate Benj. Wright		3		1		Estate of 1799 Benjamin Wright of Amherst County, son of 1767 Francis Wright of Amherst County
Jesse Wright (P Riv)	1	2		3		1850 Jesse Wright of Nelson County, son of 1799 Benjamin Wright of Amherst County and grandson of 1767 Francis Wright of Amherst County

1927(102507)

Appendix: Amherst County, Virginia, 1807 Personal Property Tax List

Lexington Parish:

Persons Names	White Tithes	Negro Tithes	Negr. betw. 12 & 16	Horses	Ridg Cariages & Stud Horses	Identification
Isaac Wright	2	2		3		1807 Isaac Wright of Amherst County, son of 1767 Francis Wright of Amherst County
Morriss Wright	1			3		Morris Wright, son of 1807 Isaac Wright of Amherst County and grandson of 1767 Francis Wright of Amherst County
Moses Wright	1		1	2		1830 Moses Wright of Amherst County, son of 1799 Benjamin Wright of Amherst County and grandson of 1767 Francis Wright of Amherst County
John Wright SM	1			1		John W. Wright, son of 1830 Moses Wright of Amherst County, grandson of 1799 Benjamin Wright of Amherst County, and great grandson of 1767 Francis Wright of Amherst County
Benjamin Wright	1			2		Benjamin Wright of Amherst County, son of 1830 Moses Wright of Amherst County, grandson of 1799 Benjamin Wright of Amherst County, and great grandson of 1767 Francis Wright of Amherst County

1809 PERSONAL PROPERTY TAX LIST

AMHERST COUNTY, VIRGINIA

Appendix: Amherst County, Virginia, 1809 Personal Property Tax List

Persons Names	White Tithes	Negro tithes	Negr. betw. 12 & 16	Horses	Stud Horses & Ridg Carriages	Identification
Moses Wright	3	1		2		1830 Moses Wright of Amherst County, son of 1799 Benjamin Wright of Amherst County and grandson of 1767 Francis Wright of Amherst County
John Wright	1			1		John W. Wright, son of 1830 Moses Wright of Amherst County, grandson of 1799 Benjamin Wright of Amherst County, and great grandson of 1767 Francis Wright of Amherst County
Benjamin Wright	1			1		Benjamin Wright of Amherst County, son of 1830 Moses Wright of Amherst County, grandson of 1799 Benjamin Wright of Amherst County, and great grandson of 1767 Francis Wright of Amherst County

1810 PERSONAL PROPERTY TAX LIST

AMHERST COUNTY, VIRGINIA

Appendix: Amherst County, Virginia, 1810 Personal Property Tax List

Persons Names	White tithes	Negro tithes	Negr. betw. 12 & 16	Horses	Stud Horses & Riding Carriages	Identification
Moses Wright	3	1		4		1830 Moses Wright of Amherst County, son of 1799 Benjamin Wright of Amherst County and grandson of 1767 Francis Wright of Amherst County
Moses Wright Jur	1			1		1849 Moses Wright of Nelson County, son of 1830 Moses Wright of Amherst County, grandson of 1799 Benjamin Wright of Amherst County, and great grandson of 1767 Francis Wright of Amherst County
Bennett Wright	1	1		1		1876 Bennett Crawford Wright of Missouri, son of 1807 Isaac Wright of Amherst County and grandson of 1767 Francis Wright of Amherst County
Benjamin Wright	1			1		Benjamin Wright, son of 1830 Moses Wright of Amherst County, grandson of 1799 Benjamin Wright of Amherst County, and great grandson of 1767 Francis Wright of Amherst County
John Wright	1			1		John W. Wright, son of 1830 Moses Wright of Amherst County, grandson of 1799 Benjamin Wright of Amherst County, and great grandson of 1767 Francis Wright of Amherst County

1811 PERSONAL PROPERTY TAX LIST

AMHERST COUNTY, VIRGINIA

Appendix: Amherst County, Virginia, 1811 Personal Property Tax List

Persons Names	White tithes	Negro tithes	Negroes Between 12 & 16	Horses	Stud Horses & Riding Carriages	Identification
Moses Wright Sr	2	1		2		1830 Moses Wright of Amherst County, son of 1799 Benjamin Wright of Amherst County and grandson of 1767 Francis Wright of Amherst County
Moses Wright Jr	1					1849 Moses Wright of Nelson County, son of 1830 Moses Wright of Amherst County, grandson of 1799 Benjamin Wright of Amherst County, and great grandson of 1767 Francis Wright of Amherst County
Benjamin Wright	1	2		1		Benjamin Wright, son of 1830 Moses Wright of Amherst County, grandson of 1799 Benjamin Wright of Amherst County, and great grandson of 1767 Francis Wright of Amherst County
John Wright	1			1		John W. Wright, son of 1830 Moses Wright of Amherst County, grandson of 1799 Benjamin Wright of Amherst County, and great grandson of 1767 Francis Wright of Amherst County
Moris Wright	1			1		Morris Wright, son of 1830 Moses Wright of Amherst County, grandson of 1799 Benjamin Wright of Amherst County, and great grandson of 1767 Francis Wright of Amherst County

1812 PERSONAL PROPERTY TAX LIST

AMHERST COUNTY, VIRGINIA

Appendix: Amherst County, Virginia, 1812 Personal Property Tax List

Persons Charged	White Tithes	Negro Tithes	Negroes Between 12 & 16	Horses	Stud Horses and Riding Carriages	Identification
Moses Wright Sr	1	1		2		1830 Moses Wright of Amherst County, son of 1799 Benjamin Wright of Amherst County and grandson of 1767 Francis Wright of Amherst County
Moses Wright Jr	1					1849 Moses Wright of Nelson County, son of 1830 Moses Wright of Amherst County, grandson of 1799 Benjamin Wright of Amherst County, and great grandson of 1767 Francis Wright of Amherst County
Benjamin Wright	1	2		1		Benjamin Wright, son of 1830 Moses Wright of Amherst County, grandson of 1799 Benjamin Wright of Amherst County, and great grandson of 1767 Francis Wright of Amherst County
Moses Wright SM	1					Moses Wright, son of 1830 Moses Wright of Amherst County, grandson of 1799 Benjamin Wright of Amherst County, and great grandson of 1767 Francis Wright of Amherst County

1813 PERSONAL PROPERTY TAX LIST

AMHERST COUNTY, VIRGINIA

Appendix: Amherst County, Virginia, 1813 Personal Property Tax List

Persons Names	White Tithes	Negro Tithes	Negroes between 12 & 16	Horses	Stud Horses	Pleasure Carriages	Identification
Moses Wright	1	1		2			1830 Moses Wright of Amherst County, son of 1799 Benjamin Wright of Amherst County and grandson of 1767 Francis Wright of Amherst County
Benjamin Wright	1	2		1			Benjamin Wright, son of 1830 Moses Wright of Amherst County, grandson of 1799 Benjamin Wright of Amherst County, and great grandson of 1767 Francis Wright of Amherst County
Morris Wright	1						Morris Wright, son of 1830 Moses Wright of Amherst County, grandson of 1799 Benjamin Wright of Amherst County, and great grandson of 1767 Francis Wright of Amherst County
John Wright	1			1			John W. Wright, son of 1830 Moses Wright of Amherst County, grandson of 1799 Benjamin Wright of Amherst County, and great grandson of 1767 Francis Wright of Amherst County
Moses Wright Junr.	1						1849 Moses Wright of Nelson County, son of 1830 Moses Wright of Amherst County, grandson of 1799 Benjamin Wright of Amherst County, and great grandson of 1767 Francis Wright of Amherst County

1814 PERSONAL PROPERTY TAX LIST

AMHERST COUNTY, VIRGINIA

Appendix: Amherst County, Virginia, 1814 Personal Property Tax List

Persons Names	White Tythes	Negro Tythes	Negroes between 12 & 16	Horses	Stud Horses	Identification
Benj Wright	1	2	0	2		Benjamin Wright, son of 1830 Moses Wright of Amherst County, grandson of 1799 Benjamin Wright of Amherst County, and great grandson of 1767 Francis Wright of Amherst County
Moses Wright	1	1	0	2		1830 Moses Wright of Amherst County, son of 1799 Benjamin Wright of Amherst County and grandson of 1767 Francis Wright of Amherst County
Morrice Wright	1			1		Morris Wright, son of 1830 Moses Wright of Amherst County, grandson of 1799 Benjamin Wright of Amherst County, and great grandson of 1767 Francis Wright of Amherst County
Moses Wright Jr.	1			1		1849 Moses Wright of Nelson County, son of 1830 Moses Wright of Amherst County, grandson of 1799 Benjamin Wright of Amherst County, and great grandson of 1767 Francis Wright of Amherst County
John Wright	1			1		John W. Wright, son of 1830 Moses Wright of Amherst County, grandson of 1799 Benjamin Wright of Amherst County, and great grandson of 1767 Francis Wright of Amherst County

1815 PERSONAL PROPERTY TAX LIST
AMHERST COUNTY, VIRGINIA

Appendix: Amherst County, Virginia, 1815 Personal Property Tax List

List A:

1815	White Tithes	Slaves between 9 & 12	Slaves above 12	Horses Mules &c	Heads Cattle	2 Wheel Riding Carriages	Value thereof	4 Wheel Riding Carriages	Value thereof	Mills	Yearly Value	Tanyards	Yearly Value	Free negroes a 16 & 45
Wm Wright			1	1	3									

1927(102507)

Appendix: Amherst County, Virginia, 1815 Personal Property Tax List

List A:

[continued from prior page]	Watches Silver gilt pinch-beck	Single cased gold watches	Double cased Do.	Horses in country Breeding in Value $500	Value thereof	Ice Houses	Clocks works of wood without cases	Do. works of Metal	Value thereof	Bureau secty, Book Case, &c	Chest drawers, clothes	tables & seper	Bedsteads
Wm Wright										Mahogany	Mahgy	Mahgy	Mahogony

119.

Appendix: Amherst County, Virginia, 1815 Personal Property Tax List

List A:

[continued from prior page]	Tea & card tables Mahgy	Window curtains calico &c	Window curtains silk &c	Venetian Blinds	pictures, prints, engravings &c	Looking Glasses	Dimensions	piano fortes &c	Bureau, secty, Book case not Mahgy	Ward Robe &c not Mahgy	Silver urns, coffee, & teapots	Silver pitcher tankard cup &c	Cut glass Decanters bowls &c
Wm Wright													

Appendix: Amherst County, Virginia, 1815 Personal Property Tax List

List A:

[continued from prior page]	Carpets	Value	Portraits in oil	Do in crayon	pictures gilt frames	Side-boards	Dollars Cents	Identification
Wm Wright							1.10	1851 William Wright of Amherst Coounty, probably son of William Wright, Jr., and grandson of William Wright (Amherst County)

Appendix: Amherst County, Virginia, 1815 Personal Property Tax List

List B:

Date of receiving list from Individual	Persons Names Charged with the Tax	No. of white males above 16 Years Old	Slaves Between 9 & 12 Years Old	Slaves Above 12 Years Old	Horses, Asses, Mules, Mares & Colts	Stud Horses No.	Stud Horses Rate of covering Mares	No. Heads of Cattle	Carriages 2 wheel riding Carriages	Carriages Phaetons & Stage Waggons	Carriages Public Stages	Carriages All other 4 wheel riding Carriages	Mills	Toll bridges & Ferries
Apl 11	Moses Wright jr	1			1			2						
Apl 12	Moses Wright Sr.	1		1	2			11						
Apl 12	Benjamin Wright	1		2	2			7						
Apl 20	John Wright	1			1			3						
May 9	Morris Wright	1			1									

Appendix: Amherst County, Virginia, 1815 Personal Property Tax List

List B:

Persons Names Charged with the Tax [continued from prior page]	Tan Yards	Free male negroes above 16 Years Old	Watches				Livery stables, and No. of stalls, orchards sufficient for One Horse	Horses in the country exceeding in Value $500	Ice Houses		Clocks			
			Gilt, Silver or Pinch- becks	Single cased Gold	Double cased Gold	Gold			Fee Private use	from which Ice is sold	Works of wood without case	Works of wood with case	Works Principally of Metals	Of Value between 50¢ $100	Of Value of $100 & upwards
Moses Wright jr															
Moses Wright Sr.															
Benjamin Wright															
John Wright															
Morris Wright															

1927(102507)

Appendix: Amherst County, Virginia, 1815 Personal Property Tax List

List B:

Persons Names Charged With the Tax [continued from prior page]	Coal Pitts	Printers, and the annual subscription to their Paper	Bureau, Secretary or Bookcase, chest of drawers, wardrobes, or Clothes press, dining table or separate part thereof, Bedsteads, sideboard with drawers or doors, Settee or Sopha, Chairs, Carpets, window curtains and Venetian blinds within the window of any House	Portraits, Picture, Print or Engraving, Mirror or Lookingglass Pianoforte, Harpsichord, Organ or Harp	Bureau, Secretary, or Bookcase, chest of drawers, Wardrobe, or Clothes press of any other wood than Mahogany	Urn, Coffee, or Tea pot, candlestick Lamp, Chandelier, Epergne, or Girandole, Decanter, Pitcher, Bowl, Goblett, Wash bason, Stand, or Salvis, Tankards, Cup, or Waiter
Moses Wright jr						
Moses Wright Sr.						
Benjamin Wright						
John Wright						
Morris Wright						

Appendix: Amherst County, Virginia, 1815 Personal Property Tax List

List B:

Persons Names Charged with the Tax [continued from prior page]	$ Cents	Identification
Moses Wright jr		1849 Moses Wright of Nelson County, son of 1830 Moses Wright of Amherst County, grandson of 1799 Benjamin Wright of Amherst County, and great grandson of 1767 Francis Wright of Amherst County
Moses Wright Sr.		1830 Moses Wright of Amherst County, son of 1799 Benjamin Wright of Amherst County and grandson of 1767 Francis Wright of Amherst County
Benjamin Wright		Benjamin Wright, son of 1830 Moses Wright of Amherst County, grandson of 1799 Benjamin Wright of Amherst County, and great grandson of 1767 Francis Wright of Amherst County
John Wright		John W. Wright, son of 1830 Moses Wright of Amherst County, grandson of 1799 Benjamin Wright of Amherst County, and great grandson of 1767 Francis Wright of Amherst County
Morris Wright		Morris Wright, son of 1830 Moses Wright of Amherst County, grandson of 1799 Benjamin Wright of Amherst County, and great grandson of 1767 Francis Wright of Amherst County

1816 PERSONAL PROPERTY TAX LIST

AMHERST COUNTY, VIRGINIA

Appendix: Amherst County, Virginia, 1816 Personal Property Tax List

Richard Powell District:

Date of receiving lists from Individuals	Persons Names Chargeable with the Tax	No. white males above 16 years	Blacks above 12 years old	Horses mares, colts, & Mules	2 Wheeled riding carriages & Harness belonging thereto		Coaches & Harness belonging thereto		Total Amt of Taxes	Identification
					Not exceeding in value $100.	Exceeding in value $100.	Not exceeding in value $200	Exceeding in value $200		
April 13	Thos Wright	1		1					.18	1852 Thomas H. Wright of Bedford County, son of 1810 John Wright of Bedford County and grandson of 1767 Francis Wright of Amherst County

Appendix: Amherst County, Virginia, 1816 Personal Property Tax List

List B:

Benjamin Wright	1	2
Moses Wright Jur.	1	1
Moses Wright Snr.	1	2
Jesse Wright Ju.	1	1
Morriss Wright	1	1
John Wright	1	1

1927(102507)

Appendix: Amherst County, Virginia, 1816 Personal Property Tax List

List B:

[continued from prior page]

		Identification
Benjamin Wright	1.06	Benjamin Wright, son of 1830 Moses Wright of Amherst County, grandson of 1799 Benjamin Wright of Amherst County, and great grandson of 1767 Francis Wright of Amherst County
Moses Wright Jur.	.18	1849 Moses Wright of Nelson County, son of 1830 Moses Wright of Amherst County, grandson of 1799 Benjamin Wright of Amherst County, and great grandson of 1767 Francis Wright of Amherst County
Moses Wright Snr.	1.06	1830 Moses Wright of Amherst County, son of 1799 Benjamin Wright of Amherst County and grandson of 1767 Francis Wright of Amherst County
Jesse Wright Ju.	.18	1873 Jesse Wright of Amherst County, son of 1830 Moses Wright of Amherst County, grandson of 1799 Benjamin Wright of Amherst County, and great grandson of 1767 Francis Wright of Amherst County
Morriss Wright	.18	Morris Wright, son of 1830 Moses Wright of Amherst County, grandson of 1799 Benjamin Wright of Amherst County, and great grandson of 1767 Francis Wright of Amherst County
John Wright	.18	John W. Wright, son of 1830 Moses Wright of Amherst County, grandson of 1799 Benjamin Wright of Amherst County, and great grandson of 1767 Francis Wright of Amherst County

1817 PERSONAL PROPERTY TAX LIST
AMHERST COUNTY, VIRGINIA

Appendix: Amherst County, Virginia, 1817 Personal Property Tax List

List A:

	Identification

[No Wrights listed]

1927(102507)

Appendix: Amherst County, Virginia, 1817 Personal Property Tax List

List B:

Persons Names	Free Males Over 16	Slaves between 12 & 16	Slaves over 16	Horses	Stud Horses	Rate p. Season	Gigs	Value	Four Wheel Carriages	Value	Amt of Tax	Identification
Benjamin Wright	1		1	1							.88	Benjamin Wright, son of 1830 Moses Wright of Amherst County, grandson of 1799 Benjamin Wright of Amherst County, and great grandson of 1767 Francis Wright of Amherst County
Moses Wright	1		1	2							1.06	1830 Moses Wright of Amherst County, son of 1799 Benjamin Wright of Amherst County and grandson of 1767 Francis Wright of Amherst County
Morriss Wright	1			1							.18	Morris Wright, son of 1830 Moses Wright of Amherst County, grandson of 1799 Benjamin Wright of Amherst County, and great grandson of 1767 Francis Wright of Amherst County
Jesse Wright Jur	1			1							.18	1873 Jesse Wright of Amherst County, son of 1830 Moses Wright of Amherst County, grandson of 1799 Benjamin Wright of Amherst County, and great grandson of 1767 Francis Wright of Amherst County
John Wright	1			1							.18	John W. Wright, son of 1830 Moses Wright of Amherst County, grandson of 1799 Benjamin Wright of Amherst County, and great grandson of 1767 Francis Wright of Amherst County

1927(102507)

Appendix: Amherst County, Virginia, 1817 Personal Property Tax List

List B:

Persons Names	Free Males Over 16	Slaves between 12 & 16	Slaves over 16	Horses	Stud Horses	Rate p. Season	Gigs	Value	Four Wheel Carriages	Value	Amt of Tax	Identification
Moses Wright Ju	1			1							.18	1849 Moses Wright of Nelson County, son of 1830 Moses Wright of Amherst County, grandson of 1799 Benjamin Wright of Amherst County, and great grandson of 1767 Francis Wright of Amherst County

1818 PERSONAL PROPERTY TAX LIST
AMHERST COUNTY, VIRGINIA

Appendix: Amherst County, Virginia, 1818 Personal Property Tax List

Richard Powell District:

Persons Names chargeable with Tax	No. white Males above 16 yrs Old	No. Slaves between 12 & 16 years old	No. Slaves above 16 years	No. Horses	2 Wheeled Riding Carriages & Harness belonging thereto		Coaches & harness belonging thereto		Total Amt of Tax $ cts	Identification
					Not exceeding in value $100	Exceeding in value $100	Not exceeding in value $200	Exceeding in value $200		

[No Wrights listed]

Appendix: Amherst County, Virginia, 1818 Personal Property Tax List

2nd Hundred:

Persons Names	Free Males Over 16	Slaves betw. 12 & 16	Slaves over 16	Horses	Stud Horses	Rate P Season	Gigs	Value	4 Wheel Carriages	Value	Amount of Tax	Identification
Moses Wright	1		1	3							1.24	1830 Moses Wright of Amherst County, son of 1799 Benjamin Wright of Amherst County and grandson of 1767 Francis Wright of Amherst County
John Wright	1			1							.18	John W. Wright, son of 1830 Moses Wright of Amherst County, grandson of 1799 Benjamin Wright of Amherst County, and great grandson of 1767 Francis Wright of Amherst County
Morriss Wright	1			1							.18	Morris Wright, son of 1830 Moses Wright of Amherst County, grandson of 1799 Benjamin Wright of Amherst County, and great grandson of 1767 Francis Wright of Amherst County
Moses Wright Jur	1			1							.18	1849 Moses Wright of Nelson County, son of 1830 Moses Wright of Amherst County, grandson of 1799 Benjamin Wright of Amherst County, and great grandson of 1767 Francis Wright of Amherst County
Jesse Wright	1			1							.18	1873 Jesse Wright of Amherst County, son of 1830 Moses Wright of Amherst County, grandson of 1799 Benjamin Wright of Amherst County, and great grandson of 1767 Francis Wright of Amherst County

1927(102507)

1819 PERSONAL PROPERTY TAX LIST

AMHERST COUNTY, VIRGINIA

Appendix: Amherst County, Virginia, 1819 Personal Property Tax List

1st 100, Addison Taliafero District:

Names of Persons	White Tithes	Negroes over 16 years	Negroes between 12 & 16	No. of Horses	Stud Horses	Rate per Season	4 Wheeled Carriages	Value	Giggs	Value	Amt Value of Tax	Identification
John W Wright	1											John W. Wright, son of 1830 Moses Wright of Amherst County, grandson of 1799 Benjamin Wright of Amherst County, and great grandson of 1767 Francis Wright of Amherst County
Wiatt Wright	1	1		1							.88	

Appendix: Amherst County, Virginia, 1819 Personal Property Tax List

2nd Hundred:

Persons Names	Free Males over 16	Slaves betw. 12 & 16	Slaves over 16	Horses	Horses &c	Stud Rate P. Season	Four Wheel Carriages	Value thereof	Gigs	Value thereof	Amount of Tax	Identification
Moses Wright Jur	1			1							.18	1849 Moses Wright of Nelson County, son of 1830 Moses Wright of Amherst County, grandson of 1799 Benjamin Wright of Amherst County, and great grandson of 1767 Francis Wright of Amherst County
John Wright (S. Moses)	1			2							.36	John W. Wright, son of 1830 Moses Wright of Amherst County, grandson of 1799 Benjamin Wright of Amherst County, and great grandson of 1767 Francis Wright of Amherst County
Benjamin Wright	1		1	2							1.06	Benjamin Wright, son of 1830 Moses Wright of Amherst County, grandson of 1799 Benjamin Wright of Amherst County, and great grandson of 1767 Francis Wright of Amherst County
Morriss Wright	1			1							.18	Morris Wright, son of 1830 Moses Wright of Amherst County, grandson of 1799 Benjamin Wright of Amherst County, and great grandson of 1767 Francis Wright of Amherst County
Moses Wright Senr	2		1	3							1.24	1830 Moses Wright of Amherst County, son of 1799 Benjamin Wright of Amherst County and grandson of 1767 Francis Wright of Amherst County

Appendix: Amherst County, Virginia, 1819 Personal Property Tax List

2nd Hundred:

Persons Names	Free Males over 16	Slaves betw. 12 & 16	Slaves over 16	Horses	Horses &c	Stud Rate P. Season	Four Wheel Carriages	Value thereof	Gigs	Value thereof	Amount of Tax	Identification
Jesse Wright	1			2							.36	1873 Jesse Wright of Amherst County, son of 1830 Moses Wright of Amherst County, grandson of 1799 Benjamin Wright of Amherst County, and great grandson of 1767 Francis Wright of Amherst County
John Wright	1											

1820 PERSONAL PROPERTY TAX LIST

AMHERST COUNTY, VIRGINIA

Appendix: Amherst County, Virginia, 1820 Personal Property Tax List

Addison Taliafero District:

dates of receiving lists of Individuals	Persons Names chargeable with Tax	No of white males above 16	Blacks above 16 ys old	Blacks between 12 & 16	Horses mares Colts & Mules	Ordinary Licence	Licence for keeping the use from last mentioned	Whole Sale and retail Merchants	Retail Merchts	Free negroes & Mulattoes	horses & Jack Asses	covering pr Season	Coaches charriots and post chaises

[No Wrights listed]

Appendix: Amherst County, Virginia, 1820 Personal Property Tax List

Addison Taliafero District:

Persons Names chargeable with Tax [continued from prior page]	Value	4 wheel carriges	Value	Giggs	Value	Amt. of Tax	Identification

[No Wrights listed]

Appendix: Amherst County, Virginia, 1820 Personal Property Tax List

2nd Hundred:

Name of Persons	Free Males over 16	Slaves between 12 & 16	Slaves over 16	Horses &c	Stud Horses &c	Rate the Season	Four Wheel Carriages	Value	Gigs	Value	Amount of Tax	Identification

[Missing list]

1821 PERSONAL PROPERTY TAX LIST

AMHERST COUNTY, VIRGINIA

Appendix: Amherst County, Virginia, 1821 Personal Property Tax List

Date of Receiving Lists	Persons Names Chargeable With Tax Book the 4th	Slaves above 12 years of age	Horses Mares Colts & Mules	Stud Horses	they Cover the Season	4 Wheel Riding Carriages &c	Value of Carriage	2 Wheel Carriages &c	Value of Carriage	Amount of Tax	Identification
	Thomas Wright	1	1							.67	1852 Thomas H. Wright of Bedford County, son of 1810 John Wright of Bedford County and grandson of 1767 Francis Wright of Amherst County
	John Wright		2							.27	John W. Wright, son of 1830 Moses Wright of Amherst County, grandson of 1799 Benjamin Wright of Amherst County, and great grandson of 1767 Francis Wright of Amherst County
__ 27	Moses Wright Ju		1							.14	1849 Moses Wright of Nelson County, son of 1830 Moses Wright of Amherst County, grandson of 1799 Benjamin Wright of Amherst County, and great grandson of 1767 Francis Wright of Amherst County
__ 28	Jesse Wright		1							.14	1873 Jesse Wright of Amherst County, son of 1830 Moses Wright of Amherst County, grandson of 1799 Benjamin Wright of Amherst County, and great grandson of 1767 Francis Wright of Amherst County
Mar 1	Moses Wright Senr.	1	2							.80	1830 Moses Wright of Amherst County, son of 1799 Benjamin Wright of Amherst County and grandson of 1767 Francis Wright of Amherst County

1927(102507)

Appendix: Amherst County, Virginia, 1821 Personal Property Tax List

Date of Receiving Lists	Persons Names Chargeable With Tax Book the 4th	Slaves above 12 years of age	Horses Mares Colts & Mules	Stud Horses	they Cover the Season	4 Wheel Riding Carriages &c	Value of Carriage	2 Wheel Carriages &c	Value of Carriage	Amount of Tax	Identification
Mar 1	Benjamin Wright	2	2							1.33	Benjamin Wright, son of 1830 Moses Wright of Amherst County, grandson of 1799 Benjamin Wright of Amherst County, and great grandson of 1767 Francis Wright of Amherst County

Appendix: Amherst County, Virginia, 1821 Personal Property Tax List

Date of Receiving Lists	Persons Names Chargeable With Tax Book the 4th	Slaves above 12 years of age	Horses Mares Colts & Mules	Stud Horses	they Cover the Season	4 Wheel Riding Carriages &c	Value of Carriage	2 Wheel Carriages &c	Value of Carriage	Amount of Tax	Identification
May 28	Morris Wright		1							.14	Morris Wright, son of 1830 Moses Wright of Amherst County, grandson of 1799 Benjamin Wright of Amherst County, and great grandson of 1767 Francis Wright of Amherst County

1822 PERSONAL PROPERTY TAX LIST
AMHERST COUNTY, VIRGINIA

Appendix: Amherst County, Virginia, 1822 Personal Property Tax List

Date of Receiving Lists	Persons Names Chargeable With Tax	Slaves above 12	Horses Mares &c	Stud Horses &c	Rate the Season	4 Wheel Carriages	Value of Carriages and Harness	2 Wheel Carriages	Value of &c	Amount of Tax	Identification
Mar 18	Thomas Wright	1	1							.67	1852 Thomas H. Wright of Bedford County, son of 1810 John Wright of Bedford County and grandson of 1767 Francis Wright of Amherst County
Apl 10	John Wright		2							.27	John W. Wright, son of 1830 Moses Wright of Amherst County, grandson of 1799 Benjamin Wright of Amherst County, and great grandson of 1767 Francis Wright of Amherst County
Apl 15	Moses Wright Sen	1	2							.80	1830 Moses Wright of Amherst County, son of 1799 Benjamin Wright of Amherst County and grandson of 1767 Francis Wright of Amherst County
Apl 15	Moses Wright Jun		1							.14	1849 Moses Wright of Nelson County, son of 1830 Moses Wright of Amherst County, grandson of 1799 Benjamin Wright of Amherst County, and great grandson of 1767 Francis Wright of Amherst County
Apl 15	Morriss Wright		1							.14	Morris Wright, son of 1830 Moses Wright of Amherst County, grandson of 1799 Benjamin Wright of Amherst County, and great grandson of 1767 Francis Wright of Amherst County

Appendix: Amherst County, Virginia, 1822 Personal Property Tax List

Date of Receiving Lists	Persons Names Chargeable With Tax	Slaves above 12	Horses Mares &c	Stud Horses &c	Rate the Season	4 Wheel Carriages	Value of Carriages and Harness	2 Wheel Carriages	Value of &c	Amount of Tax	Identification
Apl 15	Jesse Wright		1							.14	1873 Jesse Wright of Amherst County, son of 1830 Moses Wright of Amherst County, grandson of 1799 Benjamin Wright of Amherst County, and great grandson of 1767 Francis Wright of Amherst County
May 20	Benjamin Wright	2	2							1.33	Benjamin Wright, son of 1830 Moses Wright of Amherst County, grandson of 1799 Benjamin Wright of Amherst County, and great grandson of 1767 Francis Wright of Amherst County

1823 PERSONAL PROPERTY TAX LIST

AMHERST COUNTY, VIRGINIA

Appendix: Amherst County, Virginia, 1823 Personal Property Tax List

Date of Receiving Lists	Persons Names Charged With Tax	Slaves	Horses &c	Stud Horses	Rate the Season	Carriages and their Value	Total Amount of Tax	Identification
March 18	Thomas Wright	1					.47	1852 Thomas H. Wright of Bedford County, son of 1810 John Wright of Bedford County and grandson of 1767 Francis Wright of Amherst County
May 1	Moses Wright Senr		1				.12	1830 Moses Wright of Amherst County, son of 1799 Benjamin Wright of Amherst County and grandson of 1767 Francis Wright of Amherst County
May 1	Morriss Wright		1				.12	Morris Wright, son of 1830 Moses Wright of Amherst County, grandson of 1799 Benjamin Wright of Amherst County, and great grandson of 1767 Francis Wright of Amherst County
May 1	Jesse Wright		1				.12	1873 Jesse Wright of Amherst County, son of 1830 Moses Wright of Amherst County, grandson of 1799 Benjamin Wright of Amherst County, and great grandson of 1767 Francis Wright of Amherst County
May 1	Cary Wright		1				.12	Cary Wright, son of 1830 Moses Wright of Amherst County, grandson of 1799 Benjamin Wright of Amherst County, and great grandson of 1767 Francis Wright of Amherst County
May 1	Benjamin Wright	1	2				.71	Benjamin Wright, son of 1830 Moses Wright of Amherst County, grandson of 1799 Benjamin Wright of Amherst County, and great grandson of 1767 Francis Wright of Amherst County
May 1	John Wright		2				.24	John W. Wright, son of 1830 Moses Wright of Amherst County, grandson of 1799 Benjamin Wright of Amherst County, and great grandson of 1767 Francis Wright of Amherst County

1824 PERSONAL PROPERTY TAX LIST

AMHERST COUNTY, VIRGINIA

Appendix: Amherst County, Virginia, 1824 Personal Property Tax List

Date of Receiving Lists	Persons Names Chargeable With Tax	Slaves	Horses	Stud Horses	Rate of Tax	Riding Carriages of Different Descriptions and the Value	Total amount of Tax	Identification
Apr 27	Lewis Wright		1				.12	1860 Lewis Wright of Lynchburg
Apl 23	John Wright		1				.12	John W. Wright, son of 1830 Moses Wright of Amherst County, grandson of 1799 Benjamin Wright of Amherst County, and great grandson of 1767 Francis Wright of Amherst County
— 19	Jesse Wright		1				.12	1873 Jesse Wright of Amherst County, son of 1830 Moses Wright of Amherst County, grandson of 1799 Benjamin Wright of Amherst County, and great grandson of 1767 Francis Wright of Amherst County
— 19	Moses Wright Ju.		1				.12	1849 Moses Wright of Nelson County, son of 1830 Moses Wright of Amherst County, grandson of 1799 Benjamin Wright of Amherst County, and great grandson of 1767 Francis Wright of Amherst County
— 19	Cary Wright		1				.12	Cary Wright, son of 1830 Moses Wright of Amherst County, grandson of 1799 Benjamin Wright of Amherst County, and great grandson of 1767 Francis Wright of Amherst County
— 19	Benjamin Wright	1	2				.71	Benjamin Wright, son of 1830 Moses Wright of Amherst County, grandson of 1799 Benjamin Wright of Amherst County, and great grandson of 1767 Francis Wright of Amherst County
— 26	Thomas Wright	2	1				1.06	1852 Thomas H. Wright of Bedford County, son of 1810 John Wright of Bedford County and grandson of 1767 Francis Wright of Amherst County

1825 PERSONAL PROPERTY TAX LIST

AMHERST COUNTY, VIRGINIA

Appendix: Amherst County, Virginia, 1825 Personal Property Tax List

		Slaves	Horses	Stud Horses	Rate the Season	Four Wheel Riding Carriages Carryalls and Gigs and the Value thereof	Amount of Tax	Identification
Apl. 18	William Wright	3	1				1.53	1851 William Wright of Amherst County, probably son of William Wright, Jr., and grandson of William Wright (Amherst County)
Apl. 18	James Wright	1	3				.83	James Wright, son of Benjamin Wright of Amherst County, grandson of 1830 Moses Wright of Amherst County, great grandson of 1799 Benjamin Wright of Amherst County, and great great grandson of 1767 Francis Wright of Amherst County
Apl. 28	Richard J Wright		1				.12	1858 Richard Jordan Wright of Rockbridge County, son of 1804 Jordan Wright of Amherst County and grandson of Parmenos Wright
Apl. 22	John Wright		1				.12	John W. Wright, son of 1830 Moses Wright of Amherst County, grandson of 1799 Benjamin Wright of Amherst County, and great grandson of 1767 Francis Wright of Amherst County
Apl. 22	Jesse Wright Jur		1				.12	1873 Jesse Wright of Amherst County, son of 1830 Moses Wright of Amherst County, grandson of 1799 Benjamin Wright of Amherst County, and great grandson of 1767 Francis Wright of Amherst County
Apl. 22	Cary Wright		1				.12	Cary Wright, son of 1830 Moses Wright of Amherst County, grandson of 1799 Benjamin Wright of Amherst County, and great grandson of 1767 Francis Wright of Amherst County
Apl. 22	Moses Wright		1				.12	1849 Moses Wright of Nelson County, son of 1830 Moses Wright of Amherst County, grandson of 1799 Benjamin Wright of Amherst County, and great grandson of 1767 Francis Wright of Amherst County

Appendix: Amherst County, Virginia, 1825 Personal Property Tax List

		Slaves	Horses	Stud Horses	Rate the Season	Four Wheel Riding Carriages Carryalls and Gigs and the Value thereof	Amount of Tax	Identification
Apl. 22	Lavina Wright		1				.12	Lavinia (_____) Wright, widow of 1804 Jordan Wright of Amherst County, a son of Parmenos Wright
Apl. 27	Harrison Wright	3	1				1.53	1861 Harrison Wright of Rockbridge County

1927(102507)

1826 PERSONAL PROPERTY TAX LIST

AMHERST COUNTY, VIRGINIA

Appendix: Amherst County, Virginia, 1826 Personal Property Tax List

Date of Receiving Lists of Property	Persons Names Chargeable With Taxes	Slaves	Horses Mules &c	Stud Horses &c	Rate the Season	Riding Carriages Phaetons Stage Waggons, Carry Alls,& Gigs and the Value thereof	Amount of Taxes	Identification
Mar 14	Lavina Wright		1				.12	Lavinia (_____) Wright, widow of 1804 Jordan Wright of Amherst County, a son of Parmenos Wright
—	James Wright	3	2				1.65	James Wright, son of Benjamin Wright of Amherst County, grandson of 1830 Moses Wright of Amherst County, great grandson of 1799 Benjamin Wright of Amherst County, and great great grandson of 1767 Francis Wright of Amherst County
Mar 23	Harrison Wright	1	2				.71	1861 Harrison Wright of Rockbridge County
Apl. 1	John Wright		2				.24	John W. Wright, son of 1830 Moses Wright of Amherst County, grandson of 1799 Benjamin Wright of Amherst County, and great grandson of 1767 Francis Wright of Amherst County
Apr 17	William Wright	5	1				2.47	1851 William Wright of Amherst County, probably son of William Wright, Jr., and grandson of William Wright (Amherst County)
Apr 17	Benjamin Wright		1				.12	Benjamin Wright, son of 1830 Moses Wright of Amherst County, grandson of 1799 Benjamin Wright of Amherst County, and great grandson of 1767 Francis Wright of Amherst County
May 4	Jesse Wright Jur.		1				.12	1873 Jesse Wright of Amherst County, son of 1830 Moses Wright of Amherst County, grandson of 1799 Benjamin Wright of Amherst County, and great grandson of 1767 Francis Wright of Amherst County

1927(102507)

1827 PERSONAL PROPERTY TAX LIST
AMHERST COUNTY, VIRGINIA

Appendix: Amherst County, Virginia, 1827 Personal Property Tax List

				Identification
Feby 3	Lewis Wright	2	1.18	1860 Lewis Wright of Lynchburg
March 15	Lavina Wright	1	.12	Lavinia (____) Wright, widow of 1804 Jordan Wright of Amherst County, a son of Parmenos Wright
Apl 5	Moses Wright	2	.24	1849 Moses Wright of Nelson County, son of 1830 Moses Wright of Amherst County, grandson of 1799 Benjamin Wright of Amherst County, and great grandson of 1767 Francis Wright of Amherst County
Apl 7	Jesse Wright Jur.	1	.59	1873 Jesse Wright of Amherst County, son of 1830 Moses Wright of Amherst County, grandson of 1799 Benjamin Wright of Amherst County, and great grandson of 1767 Francis Wright of Amherst County
Apl 7	Benjamin Wright	1	.12	Benjamin Wright, son of 1830 Moses Wright of Amherst County, grandson of 1799 Benjamin Wright of Amherst County, and great grandson of 1767 Francis Wright of Amherst County
Apl 16	William Wright	5	2.47	1851 William Wright of Amherst County, probably son of William Wright, Jr., and grandson of William Wright (Amherst County)
May 9	John Wright Senr	1	.12	John W. Wright, son of 1830 Moses Wright of Amherst County, grandson of 1799 Benjamin Wright of Amherst County, and great grandson of 1767 Francis Wright of Amherst County

1828 PERSONAL PROPERTY TAX LIST

AMHERST COUNTY, VIRGINIA

Appendix: Amherst County, Virginia, 1828 Personal Property Tax List

Date of Receiving Lists of Property	Persons Names Chargeable With Taxes	Slaves	Horses Mules &c	Stud Horses &c	Price the Season	Riding Gigs Carryalls &c and the Value thereof	Total Amount of Taxes	Identification
Apl. 3	Robert Wright		2				.24	
May 1	William Wright	5	1				2.47	1851 William Wright of Amherst County, probably son of William Wright, Jr., and grandson of William Wright (Amherst County)
Feby 20	Richard Wright	1	2				.71	1858 Richard Jordan Wright of Rockbridge County, son of 1804 Jordan Wright of Amherst County and grandson of Parmenos Wright
Feby 20	Lewis Wright	1	1				.59	1860 Lewis Wright of Lynchburg
Feby 28	Harrison Wright	1	1				.59	1861 Harrison Wright of Rockbridge County
Apl. 5	Jesse Wright Jur.	1					.47	1873 Jesse Wright of Amherst County, son of 1830 Moses Wright of Amherst County, grandson of 1799 Benjamin Wright of Amherst County, and great grandson of 1767 Francis Wright of Amherst County
Apl. 21	Benjamin Wright		1				.12	Benjamin Wright of Amherst County, son of 1830 Moses Wright of Amherst County, grandson of 1799 Benjamin Wright of Amherst County, and great grandson of 1767 Francis Wright of Amherst County
May 10	John Wright		1				.12	John W. Wright, son of 1830 Moses Wright of Amherst County, grandson of 1799 Benjamin Wright of Amherst County, and great grandson of 1767 Francis Wright of Amherst County

1829 PERSONAL PROPERTY TAX LIST
AMHERST COUNTY, VIRGINIA

Appendix: Amherst County, Virginia, 1829 Personal Property Tax List

Date of Receiving Lists	Persons Names Charged With Taxes	Slaves	Horses &c	Stud Horses	Rate the Season	four Wheel pleasure Carriages, Gigs, Carry-alls, Phaetons &c and the Value thereof	Identification
March 17	William Wright	4	1			1.70	1851 William Wright of Amherst County, probably son of William Wright, Jr., and grandson of William Wright (Amherst County)
March 25	Jesse Wright Jun.	1	1			.40	1873 Jesse Wright of Amherst County, son of 1830 Moses Wright of Amherst County, grandson of 1799 Benjamin Wright of Amherst County, and great grandson of 1767 Francis Wright of Amherst County
Apl. 9	Lewis Wright	1	1			.50	1860 Lewis Wright of Lynchberg
Apl. 9	Richard Wright	2	1			.90	1858 Richard Jordan Wright of Rockbridge County, son of 1804 Jordan Wright of Amherst County and grandson of Parmenos Wright
Apr 30	Lavina Wright	1				.40	Lavinia (____) Wright, widow of 1804 Jordan Wright of Amherst County, a son of Parmenos Wright
Apr 30	Benjamin Wright		1			.10	Benjamin Wright, son of 1830 Moses Wright of Amherst County, grandson of 1799 Benjamin Wright of Amherst County, and great grandson of 1767 Francis Wright of Amherst County

1830 PERSONAL PROPERTY TAX LIST
AMHERST COUNTY, VIRGINIA

Appendix: Amherst County, Virginia, 1830 Personal Property Tax List

date of Receiving Lists	Persons Names Charged With Taxes	Slaves	Horses Mules &c	Stud Horses &c	Rate the Season	Carryalls, and gigs &c and the Value thereof	Total Amount of Taxes	Identification
Feby 15	William Wright	4	2				1.56	1851 William Wright of Amherst County, probably son of William Wright, Jr., and grandson of William Wright (Amherst County)
March 27	Richard Wright		1				.08	1858 Richard Jordan Wright of Rockbridge County, son of 1804 Jordan Wright of Amherst County and grandson of Parmenos Wright

[Possible missing page]

1831 PERSONAL PROPERTY TAX LIST
AMHERST COUNTY, VIRGINIA

Appendix: Amherst County, Virginia, 1831 Personal Property Tax List

Date of Receiving Lists	Persons Names Charged With Taxes	Slaves	Horses Mules &c	Stud Horses &c	Rate the Season	Four wheel Carriages Carryalls, and Gigs and the Value Thereof	Total amt of Taxes	Identification
Febry 21	William Wright, Revd.	4	2				1.12	1851 William Wright of Amherst County, probably son of William Wright, Jr., and grandson of William Wright (Amherst County)
Apl 26	Lewis Wright		1				.06	1860 Lewis Wright of Lynchburg
Apl 26	Joseph Wright	2					.50	1877 Joseph Wright of Bedford County
May 4	William Wright Trustee for Susannah Alfred	1	1				.25	
May 19	Shelton Wright & William Wright	3					.75	1874 Shelton Wright of Nelson County, son of 1850 Jesse Wright of Nelson County, grandson of 1799 Benjamin Wright of Amherst County, and great grandson of 1767 Francis Wright of Amherst County and 1870 William Wright of Amherst County, son of 1850 Jesse Wright of Nelson County, grandson of 1799 Benjamin Wright of Amherst County, and great grandson of 1767 Francis Wright of Amherst County
May 20	Jesse Wright Junr.		1				.06	1873 Jesse Wright of Amherst County, son of 1830 Moses Wright of Amherst County, grandson of 1799 Benjamin Wright of Amherst County, and great grandson of 1767 Francis Wright of Amherst County
May 20	Benjamin Wright		1				.06	Benjamin Wright, son of 1830 Moses Wright of Amherst County, grandson of 1799 Benjamin Wright of Amherst County, and great grandson of 1767 Francis Wright of Amherst County

1832 PERSONAL PROPERTY TAX LIST
AMHERST COUNTY, VIRGINIA

Appendix: Amherst County, Virginia, 1832 Personal Property Tax List

Date of Receiving Lists	Persons Names Charged With Taxes	Slaves	Horses &c	Stud Horses &c	Rate the Season	Four wheel Riding Carriages Carryalls, and Gigs and the Value Thereof	Total amt of Taxes	Identification
March 25	Joseph Wright	1					.25	1877 Joseph Wright of Bedford County
Apl 2	William Wright	3	2				.87	1851 William Wright of Amherst County, probably son of William Wright, Jr., and grandson of William Wright (Amherst County)
Apl. 2	Wm. Wright Trustee for Mary Alfred	1					.25	
March 10	William Wright	2	2				.62	1870 William Wright of Amherst County, son of 1850 Jesse Wright of Nelson County, grandson of 1799 Benjamin Wright of Amherst County, and great grandson of 1767 Francis Wright of Amherst County
March 10	Jesse Wright Jun.	1					.06	1873 Jesse Wright of Amherst County, son of 1830 Moses Wright of Amherst County, grandson of 1799 Benjamin Wright of Amherst County, and great grandson of 1767 Francis Wright of Amherst County
March 16	Benjamin Wright		1				.06	Benjamin Wright, son of 1830 Moses Wright of Amherst County, grandson of 1799 Benjamin Wright of Amherst County, and great grandson of 1767 Francis Wright of Amherst County

1833 PERSONAL PROPERTY TAX LIST
AMHERST COUNTY, VIRGINIA

Appendix: Amherst County, Virginia, 1833 Personal Property Tax List

Date of Receiving Lists	Name of Person Owning Property Chargeable With Taxes	Slaves	Horses	Studs &c	Rate the Season	Carriages Carryalls, Stage Waggons &c and the Value Thereof	Total Amount of Taxes	Identification
Feby 7	Jesse Wright Ju.		1				.06	1873 Jesse Wright of Amherst County, son of 1830 Moses Wright of Amherst County, grandson of 1799 Benjamin Wright of Amherst County, and great grandson of 1767 Francis Wright of Amherst County
Feby 18	Robert B Wright	1					.25	
March 18	William Wright	3	2				.87	1851 William Wright of Amherst County, probably son of William Wright, Jr., and grandson of William Wright (Amherst County)
March 20	William Wright	1					.25	
March 20	Charles Wright		1				.06	Charles Wright, son of Benjamin Wright of Amherst County, grandson of 1830 Moses Wright of Amherst County, great grandson of 1799 Benjamin Wright of Amherst County, and great great grandson of 1767 Francis Wright of Amherst County
March 20	James Wright		1				.06	James Wright, son of Benjamin Wright of Amherst County, grandson of 1830 Moses Wright of Amherst County, great grandson of 1799 Benjamin Wright of Amherst County, and great great grandson of 1767 Francis Wright of Amherst County
Apl. 5	Benjamin Wright		1				.06	Benjamin Wright, son of 1830 Moses Wright of Amherst County, grandson of 1799 Benjamin Wright of Amherst County, and great grandson of 1767 Francis Wright of Amherst County
Apl. 11	Joseph Wright	1	1				.31	1877 Joseph Wright of Bedford County

1834 PERSONAL PROPERTY TAX LIST

AMHERST COUNTY, VIRGINIA

Appendix: Amherst County, Virginia, 1834 Personal Property Tax List

Date of Receiving Lists of Property	Persons Names Charged With Taxes	Slaves	Horses &c	Stud Horses &c	Rate the Season	Carriages &c	Value of Carriages Gigs &c	Total Amount of Taxes	Identification
March 31	Jesse Wright Jur.		1					.06	1873 Jesse Wright of Amherst County, son of 1830 Moses Wright of Amherst County, grandson of 1799 Benjamin Wright of Amherst County, and great grandson of 1767 Francis Wright of Amherst County
Apl 22	Joseph Wright	2	1					.56	1877 Joseph Wright of Bedford County
May 19	Charles Wright		1					.06	Charles Wright, son of Benjamin Wright of Amherst County, grandson of 1830 Moses Wright of Amherst County, great grandson of 1799 Benjamin Wright of Amherst County, and great great grandson of 1767 Francis Wright of Amherst County
May 19	James Wright		1					.06	James Wright, son of Benjamin Wright of Amherst County, grandson of 1830 Moses Wright of Amherst County, great grandson of 1799 Benjamin Wright of Amherst County, and great great grandson of 1767 Francis Wright of Amherst County
May 19	Benjamin Wright		1					.06	Benjamin Wright, son of 1830 Moses Wright of Amherst County, grandson of 1799 Benjamin Wright of Amherst County, and great grandson of 1767 Francis Wright of Amherst County
May 22	William Wright	3	2					.87	1851 William Wright of Amherst County, probably son of William Wright, Jr., and grandson of William Wright (Amherst County)
May 24	Robert B. Wright	1						.25	

1835 PERSONAL PROPERTY TAX LIST

AMHERST COUNTY, VIRGINIA

Appendix: Amherst County, Virginia, 1835 Personal Property Tax List

Date of Receiving Lists	Persons Names Chargen With Taxes	Slaves	Horses &c	Stud Horses &c	Rate the Season	Riding Carriages Carryalls Gigs &c and the Value Thereof	Amount of Taxes	Identification
Feby 21	Joseph Wright	1	1				.31	1877 Joseph Wright of Bedford County
Mar. 30	Charles Wright		1				.06	Charles Wright, son of Benjamin Wright of Amherst County, grandson of 1830 Moses Wright of Amherst County, great grandson of 1799 Benjamin Wright of Amherst County, and great great grandson of 1767 Francis Wright of Amherst County
Mar. 30	Benjamin Wright		1				.06	Benjamin Wright, son of 1830 Moses Wright of Amherst County, grandson of 1799 Benjamin Wright of Amherst County, and great grandson of 1767 Francis Wright of Amherst County
Mar. 31	Shelton Wright	2					.50	1874 Shelton Wright of Nelson County, son of 1850 Jesse Wright of Nelson County, grandson of 1799 Benjamin Wright of Amherst County, and great grandson of 1767 Francis Wright of Amherst County
Mar. 31	William Wright	2	2				.62	1870 William Wright of Amherst County, son of 1850 Jesse Wright of Nelson County, grandson of 1799 Benjamin Wright of Amherst County, and great grandson of 1767 Francis Wright of Amherst County
Apl. 1	Jesse Wright Junr.		1				.06	1873 Jesse Wright of Amherst County, son of 1830 Moses Wright of Amherst County, grandson of 1799 Benjamin Wright of Amherst County, and great grandson of 1767 Francis Wright of Amherst County
Apl. 30	William Wright (Revd)	3	2				.87	1851 William Wright of Amherst County, probably son of William Wright, Jr., and grandson of William Wright (Amherst County)

1836 PERSONAL PROPERTY TAX LIST
AMHERST COUNTY, VIRGINIA

Appendix: Amherst County, Virginia, 1836 Personal Property Tax List

Date of Receiving Lists	Persons Names owning Property	Slaves	Horses &c	Studs &c	Rate the Season	Riding Carriages &c and the Value Thereof	Amount of Tax	Identification
Mar. 21	William Wright (Revd.)	3	2				.87	1851 William Wright of Amherst County, probably son of William Wright, Jr., and grandson of William Wright (Amherst County)
Apl. 8	Joseph Wright	1	1				.31	1877 Joseph Wright of Bedford County
Apl. 30	Charles Wright		3				.18	Charles Wright, son of Benjamin Wright of Amherst County, grandson of 1830 Moses Wright of Amherst County, great grandson of 1799 Benjamin Wright of Amherst County, and great great grandson of 1767 Francis Wright of Amherst County
Apl. 30	Benjamin Wright		1				.06	Benjamin Wright, son of 1830 Moses Wright of Amherst County, grandson of 1799 Benjamin Wright of Amherst County, and great grandson of 1767 Francis Wright of Amherst County
Apl. 30	William Wright	2	3				.68	1870 William Wright of Amherst County, son of 1850 Jesse Wright of Nelson County, grandson of 1799 Benjamin Wright of Amherst County, and great grandson of 1767 Francis Wright of Amherst County
Apl. 30	Shelton Wright	1	1				.31	1874 Shelton Wright of Nelson County, son of 1850 Jesse Wright of Nelson County, grandson of 1799 Benjamin Wright of Amherst County, and great grandson of 1767 Francis Wright of Amherst County
May 20	Jesse Wright Jur		1				.06	1873 Jesse Wright of Amherst County, son of 1830 Moses Wright of Amherst County, grandson of 1799 Benjamin Wright of Amherst County, and great grandson of 1767 Francis Wright of Amherst County

1927(102507)

1837 PERSONAL PROPERTY TAX LIST

AMHERST COUNTY, VIRGINIA

Appendix: Amherst County, Virginia, 1837 Personal Property Tax List

Date of Receiving Lists	Persons Names Charged with Property	Slaves	Horses &c	Stud Horses	Rate the Season	Carriages Gigs Carry-alls &c	Value thereof	Amount of Tax	Identification
Apl. 22	William Wright Revd.	3	3					.93	1851 William Wright of Amherst County, probably son of William Wright, Jr., and grandson of William Wright (Amherst County)
Apl. 22	William Wright	1	4					.49	1870 William Wright of Amherst County, son of 1850 Jesse Wright of Nelson County, grandson of 1799 Benjamin Wright of Amherst County, and great grandson of 1767 Francis Wright of Amherst County
Apl. 22	Charles Wright		3					.18	Charles Wright, son of Benjamin Wright of Amherst County, grandson of 1830 Moses Wright of Amherst County, great grandson of 1799 Benjamin Wright of Amherst County, and great great grandson of 1767 Francis Wright of Amherst County
Apl. 22	Benjamin Wright		1					.06	Benjamin Wright, son of 1830 Moses Wright of Amherst County, grandson of 1799 Benjamin Wright of Amherst County, and great grandson of 1767 Francis Wright of Amherst County
Mar. 20	Joseph Wright	1	1					.31	1877 Joseph Wright of Bedford County
Mar. 27	Jesse Wright		1					.06	1873 Jesse Wright of Amherst County, son of 1830 Moses Wright of Amherst County, grandson of 1799 Benjamin Wright of Amherst County, and great grandson of 1767 Francis Wright of Amherst County
May 1	Ambrose F. Wright	8	2					2.12	Ambrose F. Wright, son of 1823 George Wright of Campbell County and grandson of Robert Wright, Sr. (Campbell County)

1838 PERSONAL PROPERTY TAX LIST
AMHERST COUNTY, VIRGINIA

Appendix: Amherst County, Virginia, 1838 Personal Property Tax List

Date of the Lists	Persons Names	Slaves	Horses &c	Studs &c	Rate	Carriages &c	Value	Amount of Tax	Identification
Mar 20	William Wright	3	5					1.30	1870 William Wright of Amherst County, son of 1850 Jesse Wright of Nelson County, grandson of 1799 Benjamin Wright of Amherst County, and great grandson of 1767 Francis Wright of Amherst County
Mar 20	Joseph Wright	1	2					.46	1877 Joseph Wright of Bedford County
Mar 20	Ellis Wright	1	2					.46	1880 Ellis Wright of Amherst County, son of 1850 Jesse Wright of Nelson County, grandson of 1799 Benjamin Wright of Amherst County, and great grandson of 1767 Francis Wright of Amherst County
Mar 31	Jesse Wright Jur		1					.08	1873 Jesse Wright of Amherst County, son of 1830 Moses Wright of Amherst County, grandson of 1799 Benjamin Wright of Amherst County, and great grandson of 1767 Francis Wright of Amherst County
Apl. 26	William Wright (Revd.)	3	2					1.06	1851 William Wright of Amherst County, probably son of William Wright, Jr., and grandson of William Wright (Amherst County)
May 17	Benjamin Wright		1					.08	Benjamin Wright, son of 1830 Moses Wright of Amherst County, grandson of 1799 Benjamin Wright of Amherst County, and great grandson of 1767 Francis Wright of Amherst County
May 17	Charles Wright		2					.16	Charles Wright, son of Benjamin Wright of Amherst County, grandson of 1830 Moses Wright of Amherst County, great grandson of 1799 Benjamin Wright of Amherst County, and great great grandson of 1767 Francis Wright of Amherst County

1839 PERSONAL PROPERTY TAX LIST
AMHERST COUNTY, VIRGINIA

Appendix: Amherst County, Virginia, 1839 Personal Property Tax List

Date of Receiving Lists		Free Males over 16	Slaves betw. 12 & 16	Slaves over 16	Horses Mules &c	Stud Horses &c	Rate the Season	Carriages Gigs &c	The Value of Carriages Gigs &c	Amount of Tax	Identification
Apl. 2	William Wright Revd	1		3	3					1.14	1851 William Wright of Amherst County, probably son of William Wright, Jr., and grandson of William Wright (Amherst County)
May 22	Robert D Wright	1			1					.08	1873 Robert D. Wright of Amherst County, probably son of Charles Wright and grandson of Robert Wright, Sr. (Campbell County)
Mar 18	William Wright	1									
Mar 18	Lewis Wright	1									1860 Lewis Wright of Lynchburg
Mar 18	William Wright	1	1	1	4					.92	1870 William Wright of Amherst County, son of 1850 Jesse Wright of Nelson County, grandson of 1799 Benjamin Wright of Amherst County, and great grandson of 1767 Francis Wright of Amherst County
June 27	Jesse Wright Jur.	1			1					.08	1873 Jesse Wright of Amherst County, son of 1830 Moses Wright of Amherst County, grandson of 1799 Benjamin Wright of Amherst County, and great grandson of 1767 Francis Wright of Amherst County

Appendix: Amherst County, Virginia, 1839 Personal Property Tax List

Date of Receiving Lists		Free Males over 16	Slaves betw. 12 & 16	Slaves over 16	Horses Mules &c	Stud Horses &c	Rate the Season	Carriages Gigs &c	The Value of Carriages Gigs &c	Amount of Tax	Identification
June 27	Shelton Wright Jur.	1									1862 Shelton H. Wright of Amherst County, son of 1873 Jesse Wright of Amherst County, grandson of 1830 Moses Wright of Amherst County, great grandson of 1799 Benjamin Wright of Amherst County, and great great grandson of 1767 Francis Wright of Amherst County
June 27	Benjamin Wright	1			1					.08	Benjamin Wright, son of 1830 Moses Wright of Amherst County, grandson of 1799 Benjamin Wright of Amherst County, and great grandson of 1767 Francis Wright of Amherst County
June 27	Joseph Wright	1			1					.08	1877 Joseph Wright of Bedford County

1840 PERSONAL PROPERTY TAX LIST

AMHERST COUNTY, VIRGINIA

Appendix: Amherst County, Virginia, 1840 Personal Property Tax List

Date of Receiving Lists	Persons Names	Slaves	Horses &c	Studs &c	Rate Season	Pleasure Carriages Carryalls & Gigs, Value Thereof	Amount of Tax	Identification
Apl. 10	Jesse Wright Jur.		2				.16	1873 Jesse Wright of Amherst County, son of 1830 Moses Wright of Amherst County, grandson of 1799 Benjamin Wright of Amherst County, and great grandson of 1767 Francis Wright of Amherst County
Apl. 10	William Wright	2	5				1.00	1870 William Wright of Amherst County, son of 1850 Jesse Wright of Nelson County, grandson of 1799 Benjamin Wright of Amherst County, and great grandson of 1767 Francis Wright of Amherst County
Apl. 10	Ellis Wright	1	3				.54	1880 Ellis Wright of Amherst County, son of 1850 Jesse Wright of Nelson County, grandson of 1799 Benjamin Wright of Amherst County, and great grandson of 1767 Francis Wright of Amherst County
Apl. 10	Charles Wright		2				.16	Charles Wright, son of Benjamin Wright of Amherst County, grandson of 1830 Moses Wright of Amherst County, great grandson of 1799 Benjamin Wright of Amherst County, and great great grandson of 1767 Francis Wright of Amherst County
Apl. 10	Benjamin Wright		1				.08	Benjamin Wright, son of 1830 Moses Wright of Amherst County, grandson of 1799 Benjamin Wright of Amherst County, and great grandson of 1767 Francis Wright of Amherst County
Apl. 23	William Wright Revd,	3	3				1.14	1851 William Wright of Amherst County, probably son of William Wright, Jr., and grandson of William Wright (Amherst County)
Apl. 23	Joseph Wright		1				.08	1877 Joseph Wright of Bedford County

1841 PERSONAL PROPERTY TAX LIST

AMHERST COUNTY, VIRGINIA

Appendix: Amherst County, Virginia, 1841 Personal Property Tax List

Date of Receiving Lists	Name of Persons Charged With Taxes	Slaves	Horses Mules &c	Carriages Carryalls and Gigs, & Value Thereof	Identification
Mar 25	William B Wright		1	.13	
Mar 25	William Wright		1	.13	1887 William S. Wright of Gilmer County, West Virginia, probably son of Charles Wright of Decatur County, Indiana, and grandson of William Wright, Sr. (Bedford County)
Apl 19	Ellis Wright	1	1	.53	1880 Ellis Wright of Amherst County, son of 1850 Jesse Wright of Nelson County, grandson of 1799 Benjamin Wright of Amherst County, and great grandson of 1767 Francis Wright of Amherst County
Apl 19	Charles Wright		1	.13	Charles Wright, son of Benjamin Wright of Amherst County, grandson of 1830 Moses Wright of Amherst County, great grandson of 1799 Benjamin Wright of Amherst County, and great great grandson of 1767 Francis Wright of Amherst County
Apl 19	William Wright	2	3	1.18	1870 William Wright of Amherst County, son of 1850 Jesse Wright of Nelson County, grandson of 1799 Benjamin Wright of Amherst County, and great grandson of 1767 Francis Wright of Amherst County
Apl 19	Benjamin Wright		1	.13	Benjamin Wright, son of 1830 Moses Wright of Amherst County, grandson of 1799 Benjamin Wright of Amherst County, and great grandson of 1767 Francis Wright of Amherst County
Apl 19	Jesse Wright		1	.13	1873 Jesse Wright of Amherst County, son of 1830 Moses Wright of Amherst County, grandson of 1799 Benjamin Wright of Amherst County, and great grandson of 1767 Francis Wright of Amherst County
Apl 19	Shelton Wright		1	.13	1862 Shelton H. Wright of Amherst County, son of 1873 Jesse Wright of Amherst County, grandson of 1830 Moses Wright of Amherst County, great grandson of 1799 Benjamin Wright of Amherst County, and great great grandson of 1767 Francis Wright of Amherst County

Appendix: Amherst County, Virginia, 1841 Personal Property Tax List

Date of Receiving Lists	Name of Persons Charged With Taxes	Slaves	Horses Mules &c	Carriages Carryalls and Gigs, & Value Thereof	Identification
May 17	William Wright, Revd	4	4	2.10	1851 William Wright of Amherst County, probably son of William Wright, Jr., and grandson of William Wright (Amherst County)
May 17	Robert D Wright		1	.13	1873 Robert D. Wright of Amherst County, probably son of Charles Wright and grandson of Robert Wright, Sr. (Campbell County)

1842 PERSONAL PROPERTY TAX LIST

AMHERST COUNTY, VIRGINIA

Appendix: Amherst County, Virginia, 1842 Personal Property Tax List

Date of Receiving Lists	Persons Names	Slaves	Horses &c	Piano fortes	Clocks	Watches	Silver or Gold plate Carriages &c The Value of Plate & Carriages &c.	Amount of Tax	Identification
Mar 30	William S Wright		1					.13	1887 William S. Wright of Gilmer County, West Virginia, probably son of Charles Wright of Decatur County, Indiana, and grandson of William Wright, Sr. (Bedford County)
Apl 28	Jesse Wright Jur.		1					.13	1873 Jesse Wright of Amherst County, son of 1830 Moses Wright of Amherst County, grandson of 1799 Benjamin Wright of Amherst County, and great grandson of 1767 Francis Wright of Amherst County
Apl 28	Ellis Wright	1	1					.5	1880 Ellis Wright of Amherst County, son of 1850 Jesse Wright of Nelson County, grandson of 1799 Benjamin Wright of Amherst County, and great grandson of 1767 Francis Wright of Amherst County
Apl 28	William Wright	3	4					1.70	1870 William Wright of Amherst County, son of 1850 Jesse Wright of Nelson County, grandson of 1799 Benjamin Wright of Amherst County, and great grandson of 1767 Francis Wright of Amherst County
Apl 28	Shelton H Wright		1					.13	1862 Shelton H. Wright of Amherst County, son of 1873 Jesse Wright of Amherst County, grandson of 1830 Moses Wright of Amherst County, great grandson of 1799 Benjamin Wright of Amherst County, and great great grandson of 1767 Francis Wright of Amherst County

Appendix: Amherst County, Virginia, 1842 Personal Property Tax List

Date of Receiving Lists	Persons Names	Slaves	Horses &c	Piano fortes	Clocks	Watches	Silver or Gold plate Carriages &c The Value of Plate & Carriages &c.	Amount of Tax	Identification
Apl 28	Alexander Wright		1					.13	Probably 1891 Alexander Wright of Greenbrier County, West Virginia, son of Benjamin Wright, grandson of 1830 Moses Wright of Amherst County, great grandson of 1799 Benjamin Wright of Amherst County, and great great grandson of 1767 Francis Wright of Amherst County
Apl 28	Joseph Wright		1					.13	1877 Joseph Wright of Bedford County
June 3d	William B Wright		1					.13	
May 17	William Wright, (Revd)	4	4					2.15	1851 William Wright of Amherst County, probably son of William Wright, Jr., and grandson of William Wright (Amherst County)

1927(102507)

201.

1843 PERSONAL PROPERTY TAX LIST

AMHERST COUNTY, VIRGINIA

Appendix: Amherst County, Virginia, 1843 Personal Property Tax List

Date of Receiving Lists	Persons Names	Slaves	Horses &c	Money loaned out & Bonds Purchsd	Tax on the Interest of Money Loaned	Salaries and monied income over $400	Watches	Clocks	Piano Fortes	Tax on Pianoes	Conveyances	Probate of Wills
Apr 27	William Wright	3	4					1 Wood				
Apl 27	Shelton Wright	2	1					1 Wood				
Apl 28	Shelton H. Wright		1									
Apl 28	Jesse Wright Jur.		3					1 Wood				
May 6	William Wright Revd.	4	3					1 Mettle				
May 15	Joseph Wright		1									
May 15	Lewis Wright		1									
June 16	William S Wright		1									

Appendix: Amherst County, Virginia, 1843 Personal Property Tax List

Persons Names [continued from prior page]	Silver plate over 50 oz.	Tax on Plate	Carriages &c	Value of Carriages, Carryalls and Gigs	Total amt of Tax	Identification
William Wright					2.19	1870 William Wright of Amherst County, son of 1850 Jesse Wright of Nelson County, grandson of 1799 Benjamin Wright of Amherst County, and great grandson of 1767 Francis Wright of Amherst County
Shelton Wright					1.3_	1874 Shelton Wright of Nelson County, son of 1850 Jesse Wright of Nelson County, grandson of 1799 Benjamin Wright of Amherst County, and great grandson of 1767 Francis Wright of Amherst County
Shelton H. Wright					.14	1862 Shelton H. Wright of Amherst County, son of 1873 Jesse Wright of Amherst County, grandson of 1830 Moses Wright of Amherst County, great grandson of 1799 Benjamin Wright of Amherst County, and great great grandson of 1767 Francis Wright of Amherst County
Jesse Wright Jur.					.6_	1873 Jesse Wright of Amherst County, son of 1830 Moses Wright of Amherst County, grandson of 1799 Benjamin Wright of Amherst County, and great grandson of 1767 Francis Wright of Amherst County
William Wright Revd.					2.76	1851 William Wright of Amherst County, probably son of William Wright, Jr., and grandson of William Wright (Amherst County)
Joseph Wright					.14	1877 Joseph Wright of Bedford County
Lewis Wright					.14	1860 Lewis Wright of Lynchburg
William S Wright					.14	1887 William S. Wright of Gilmer County, West Virginia, probably son of Charles Wright of Decatur County, Indiana, and grandson of William Wright, Sr. (Bedford County)

1844 PERSONAL PROPERTY TAX LIST

AMHERST COUNTY, VIRGINIA

Appendix: Amherst County, Virginia, 1844 Personal Property Tax List

Date of Receiving Lists	Name of Persons Charged With Taxes	Slaves above 12 yr old	Horses &c	2 Wheel Pleasure Carriages and the Value	No. Stages and the Value	No. Carryalls and the Value	No. of 2 Wheel Carriages and the Value	No of Gold Watches	No of Patent Lever or Lapine Silver Watches	No of Other Watches	Clocks paying 50 cts	Clocks paying 25 cts
Apl 25	Shelton H Wright		1									
Apl 25	Jesse Wright Jur		2									
Apl 25	William Wright	1	2									1
May 4	Henry T Wright	1	2							1		1
	Thomas Wright											
	William Wright Revd.	4	3								1	
May 9	Ellis Wright	2	1									
June 13	William Wright		1									1

208.

Appendix: Amherst County, Virginia, 1844 Personal Property Tax List

Name of Persons Charged With Taxes [continued from prior page]	Pianoes	Gold or Silver Plate	Attornies	Physicians	Dentist	Amt. of Interest on Profits, on Money Loaned out or on Bonds acquired by Purchases &c	Amount of Monied yearly income over $400 Rec'd as salaries or fees of office	Bridges amt. of yearly Rent over $100	Ferries amt of yearly Rent over $100	No of newspaper printing Presses & amt of Tax
Shelton H Wright										
Jesse Wright Jur										
William Wright										
Henry T Wright										
Thomas Wright										
William Wright Revd.										
Ellis Wright										
William Wright										

Appendix: Amherst County, Virginia, 1844 Personal Property Tax List

Name of Persons Charged With Taxes [continued from prior page]	Deeds Probate of Wills and Letters of	Collateral Interest	Amount of Tax Dollars Cents	Identification
Shelton H Wright			.13	1862 Shelton H. Wright of Amherst County, son of 1873 Jesse Wright of Amherst County, grandson of 1830 Moses Wright of Amherst County, great grandson of 1799 Benjamin Wright of Amherst County, and great great grandson of 1767 Francis Wright of Amherst County
Jesse Wright Jur			.25	1873 Jesse Wright of Amherst County, son of 1830 Moses Wright of Amherst County, grandson of 1799 Benjamin Wright of Amherst County, and great grandson of 1767 Francis Wright of Amherst County
William Wright			.90	1870 William Wright of Amherst County, son of 1850 Jesse Wright of Nelson County, grandson of 1799 Benjamin Wright of Amherst County, and great grandson of 1767 Francis Wright of Amherst County
Henry T Wright			1.15	1914 Henry Talley Wright of Amherst County, son of William Wright (Hanover County Tailor)
Thomas Wright	1		.50	
William Wright Revd.	1		2.48	1851 William Wright of Amherst County, probably son of William Wright, Jr., and grandson of William Wright (Amherst County)
Ellis Wright			.93	1880 Ellis Wright of Amherst County, son of 1850 Jesse Wright of Nelson County, grandson of 1799 Benjamin Wright of Amherst County, and great grandson of 1767 Francis Wright of Amherst County
William Wright			.38	1887 William S. Wright of Gilmer County, West Virginia, probably son of Charles Wright of Decatur County, Indiana, and grandson of William Wright, Sr. (Bedford County)

1845 PERSONAL PROPERTY TAX LIST

AMHERST COUNTY, VIRGINIA

Appendix: Amherst County, Virginia, 1845 Personal Property Tax List

	Persons Chargeable With Tax	Whites above 16 years of age	Slaves above 15 years of age	Slaves above 12 years of age	Horses Mules &c	4 wheel pleasure carriages and harness and value	Stages, and value, including harness	Carryalls and harness, and value	2 wheel pleasure carriages and harness and Value	Gold watches	Patent lever or lapine silver watches	Other watches
Mar 12	William Wright	1			1							
Mar 14	Henry T Wright	1		1	2							1
Apl 5	Lewis Wright	2			2							
Apl. 5	Joseph Wright	1			1							
Apl. 23	Jesse Wright Jur.	1			3							
Apl 24	Ellis Wright	1	1		1							
Apl 24	William Wright	1	1		2							
May 19	Shelton H Wright	1			1							
May 21	Robert D Wright	2			1							

Appendix: Amherst County, Virginia, 1845 Personal Property Tax List

Persons Chargeable With Tax	Whites above 16 years of age	Slaves above 15 years of age	Slaves above 12 years of age	Horses Mules &c	4 wheel pleasure carriages and harness and value	Stages, and value, including harness	Carryalls and harness, and value	2 wheel pleasure carriages and harness and Value	Gold watches	Patent lever or lapine silver watches	Other watches
William Wright	1										
Henry T Wright	1										
Lewis Wright											
Joseph Wright											
Jesse Wright Jur.		1									
Ellis Wright	1										
William Wright		1									
Shelton H. Wright											
Robert D Wright											

1927(102507)

Appendix: Amherst County, Virginia, 1845 Personal Property Tax List

Persons Chargeable With Tax [continued from prior page]	Bridges-- am't of yearly rent or value over $100	Ferries- am't of yearly rent or value over $100	Newspaper printing presses and amount of tax	Total am't of tax Dollars Cents.	Identification
William Wright				.23	Probably 1887 William S. Wright of Gilmer County, West Virginia, probably son of Charles Wright of Decatur County, Indiana, and grandson of William Wright, Sr. (Bedford County)
Henry T Wright				.90	1914 Henry Talley Wright of Amherst County, son of William Wright (Hanover County Tailor)
Lewis Wright				.70	1860 Lewis Wright of Lynchburg
Joseph Wright				.10	1877 Joseph Wright of Bedford County
Jesse Wright Jur.				.43	1873 Jesse Wright of Amherst County, son of 1830 Moses Wright of Amherst County, grandson of 1799 Benjamin Wright of Amherst County, and great grandson of 1767 Francis Wright of Amherst County
Ellis Wright				.55	1880 Ellis Wright of Amherst County, son of 1850 Jesse Wright of Nelson County, grandson of 1799 Benjamin Wright of Amherst County, and great grandson of 1767 Francis Wright of Amherst County
William Wright				.65	1870 William Wright of Amherst County, son of 1850 Jesse Wright of Nelson County, grandson of 1799 Benjamin Wright of Amherst County, and great grandson of 1767 Francis Wright of Amherst County
Shelton H. Wright				.10	1862 Shelton H. Wright of Amherst County, son of 1873 Jesse Wright of Amherst County, grandson of 1830 Moses Wright of Amherst County, great grandson of 1799 Benjamin Wright of Amherst County, and great great grandson of 1767 Francis Wright of Amherst County
Robert D Wright				.10	1873 Robert D. Wright of Amherst County, probably son of Charles Wright and probably grandson of Robert Wright, Sr. (Campbell County)

1927(102507)

Appendix: Amherst County, Virginia, 1845 Personal Property Tax List

	Persons Chargeable With Tax	Whites above 16 years of age	Slaves above 15 years of age	Slaves above 12 years of age	Horses Mules &c	4 wheel pleasure carriages and harness and value	Stages, and value, including harness	Carryalls and harness, and value	2 wheel pleasure carriages and harness and Value	Gold watches	Patent lever or lapine silver watches	Other watches
May 21	Fielding Wright	1										
May 22	William Wright (Revd)	1	3		3							
May 22	Jesse K Wright	1										
May 23	Alexander Wright	1										
May 23	Benjamin Wright Jur	1										
May 23	Burwell Wright	1										

1927(102507)

Appendix: Amherst County, Virginia, 1845 Personal Property Tax List

Persons Chargeable With Tax [continued from prior page]	Metallic clocks	Other Clocks	Pianos and value	Plate over the value of $50	Attornies paying specific tax, and am't of tax	Physicians and surgeons paying specific tax, and amount of tax	Dentists paying specific tax, and amount of tax	Am't of int. of profits on moneys loaned out, or on bonds acquired by purchase, including interest, profits, or dividends, on state or corporat'n bonds	Am't of monied yearly income over $400 received as salaries or as fees of office
Fielding Wright									
William Wright (Revd)		1							
Jesse K Wright									
Alexander Wright									
Benjamin Wright Jur									
Burwell Wright									

Appendix: Amherst County, Virginia, 1845 Personal Property Tax List

Persons Chargeable With Tax [continued from prior page]	Bridges-- am't of yearly rent or value over $100	Ferries-- am't of yearly rent or value over $100	Newspaper printing presses and amount of tax	Total am't of tax Dollars Cents.	Identification
Fielding Wright					Fielding Hobson Wright, son of 1873 Robert D. Wright of Amherst County, probably grandson of Charles Wright, and probably great grandson of Robert Wright, Sr. (Campbell County)
William Wright (Revd)				1.39	1851 William Wright of Amherst County, probably son of William Wright, Jr., and grandson of William Wright (Amherst County)
Jesse K Wright					1855 Jesse K. Wright of Nelson County, son of 1851 William Wright of Amherst County, probably grandson of William Wright, Jr., and great grandson of William Wright (Amherst County)
Alexander Wright					Probably 1891 Alexander Wright of Greenbrier County, West Virginia, son of Benjamin Wright, grandson of 1830 Moses Wright of Amherst County, great grandson of 1799 Benjamin Wright of Amherst County, and great great grandson of 1767 Francis Wright of Amherst County
Benjamin Wright Jur					Benjamin Wright, son of Benjamin Wright, grandson of 1830 Moses Wright of Amherst County, great grandson of 1799 Benjamin Wright of Amherst County, and great great grandson of 1767 Francis Wright of Amherst County
Burwell Wright					

1846 PERSONAL PROPERTY TAX LIST

AMHERST COUNTY, VIRGINIA

Appendix: Amherst County, Virginia, 1846 Personal Property Tax List

Persons Chargeable With Tax		Whites above 16 years of age	Slaves above 15 years of age	Slaves above 12 years of age	Horses Mules &c	4 wheel pleasure carriages and harness and value	Stages, and value, including harness	Carryalls and harness, and value	2 wheel pleasure carriages and harness and Value	Gold watches	Patent lever or lapine silver watches	Other watches
April 23	Lewis Wright	2			2							
May 1	Thomas Wright		1	1								
May 6	William B Wright	1										
May 9	Jesse Wright	1										
May 9	William Wright	1	3		2							
May 18	Henry T Wright	1			2						1	
May 21	Robert Wright	2			1							
June 10	Fielding H Wright	1										
July 1	William Wright	1	1		2							
July 1	Ellis Wright	1	1		2							

Appendix: Amherst County, Virginia, 1846 Personal Property Tax List

Persons Chargeable With Tax [continued from prior page]	Metallic clocks	Other Clocks	Pianos and value	Plate over the value of $50	Attornies paying specific tax, and am't of tax	Physicians and surgeons paying specific tax, and amount of tax	Dentists paying specific tax, and amount of tax	Am't of int. of profits on moneys loaned out, or on bonds acquired by purchase, including interest, profits, or dividends, on state or corporat'n bonds	Am't of monied yearly income over $400 received as salaries or as fees of office
Lewis Wright									
Thomas Wright									
William B Wright	1								
Jesse Wright									
William Wright		1							
Henry T Wright	1								
Robert Wright									
Fielding H Wright									
William Wright		1							
Ellis Wright		1							

Appendix: Amherst County, Virginia, 1846 Personal Property Tax List

Persons Chargeable With Tax [continued from prior page]	Bridges- am't of yearly rent or value over $100	Ferries- am't of yearly rent or value over $100	Newspaper printing presses and amount of tax	Total am't of tax Dollars Cents	Identification
Lewis Wright				.20	1860 Lewis Wright of Lynchburg
Thomas Wright				.13	
William B Wright					
Jesse Wright					Probably 1855 Jesse K. Wright of Nelson County, son of 1851 William Wright of Amherst County, probably son of William Wright, Jr., and grandson of William Wright (Amherst County)
William Wright				1.41	1851 William Wright of Amherst County, probably son of William Wright, Jr., and grandson of William Wright (Amherst County)
Henry T Wright				1.58	1914 Henry Talley Wright of Amherst County, son of William Wright (Hanover County Tailor)
Robert Wright				.10	1873 Robert D. Wright of Amherst County, probably son of Charles Wright and probably grandson of Robert Wright, Sr. (Campbell County)
Fielding Wright					Fielding Hobson Wright, son of 1873 Robert D. Wright of Amherst County, probably grandson of Charles Wright, and probably great grandson of Robert Wright, Sr. (Campbell County)
William Wright				.77	1870 William Wright of Amherst County, son of 1850 Jesse Wright of Nelson County, grandson of 1799 Benjamin Wright of Amherst County, and great grandson of 1767 Francis Wright of Amherst County
Ellis Wright				.77	1880 Ellis Wright of Amherst County, son of 1850 Jesse Wright of Nelson County, grandson of 1799 Benjamin Wright of Amherst County, and great grandson of 1767 Francis Wright of Amherst County

Appendix: Amherst County, Virginia, 1846 Personal Property Tax List

	Persons Chargeable With Tax	Whites above 16 years of age	Slaves above 15 years of age	Slaves above 12 years of age	Horses Mules &c	4 wheel pleasure carriages and harness and value	Stages, and value, including harness	Carryalls and harness, and value	2 wheel pleasure carriages and harness and Value	Gold watches	Patent lever or lapine silver watches	Other watches
July 1	Benjamin Wright jr	1			1							
July 1	Benjamin Wright Snr	1			1							
July 1	Jesse Wright jr	1			1							
July 1	Shelton Wright	1			1							

Appendix: Amherst County, Virginia, 1846 Personal Property Tax List

Persons Chargeable With Tax [continued from prior page]	Metallic clocks	Other Clocks	Pianos and value	Plate over the value of $50	Attornies paying specific tax, and am't of tax	Physicians and surgeons paying specific tax, and amount of tax	Dentists paying specific tax, and amount of tax	Am't of int. of profits on moneys loaned out, or on bonds acquired by purchase, including interest, profits, or dividends, on state or corporat'n bonds	Am't of monied yearly income over $400 received as salaries or as fees of office
Benjamin Wright jr		1							
Benjamin Wright Snr									
Jesse Wright jr			1						
Shelton Wright									

Appendix: Amherst County, Virginia, 1846 Personal Property Tax List

Persons Chargeable With Tax [continued from prior page]	Bridges- am't of yearly rent or value over $100	Ferries- am't of yearly rent or value over $100	Newspaper printing presses and amount of tax	Total am't of tax Dollars Cents	Identification
Benjamin Wright jr				.35	Benjamin Wright, son of Benjamin Wright, grandson of 1830 Moses Wright of Amherst County, great grandson of 1799 Benjamin Wright of Amherst County, and great great grandson of 1767 Francis Wright of Amherst County
Benjamin Wright Snr				.10	Benjamin Wright, son of 1830 Moses Wright of Amherst County, grandson of 1799 Benjamin Wright of Amherst County, and great grandson of 1767 Francis Wright of Amherst County
Jesse Wright jr				.23	1873 Jesse Wright of Amherst County, son of 1830 Moses Wright of Amherst County, grandson of 1799 Benjamin Wright of Amherst County, and great grandson of 1767 Francis Wright of Amherst County
Shelton Wright				.10	1862 Shelton H. Wright of Amherst County, son of 1873 Jesse Wright of Amherst County, grandson of 1830 Moses Wright of Amherst County, great grandson of 1799 Benjamin Wright of Amherst County, and great great grandson of 1767 Francis Wright of Amherst County

226.

1847 PERSONAL PROPERTY TAX LIST

AMHERST COUNTY, VIRGINIA

Appendix: Amherst County, Virginia, 1847 Personal Property Tax List

	Persons Chargeable With Tax	Whites above 16 years of age	Slaves above 15 years of age	Slaves above 12 years of age	Horses Mules &c	4 wheel pleasure carriages and harness and value	Stages, and value, including harness	Carryalls and harness, and value	2 wheel pleasure carriages and harness and Value	Gold watches	Patent lever or lapine silver watches	Other watches
Feby 15	Henry T Wright	1	1		1							1
Feby 20	Thomas Wright		3									
Mar 4	Lewis Wright	2			2							
Mar 25	Fielding H Wright	1	1									
Mar 26	Shelton H Wright	1	1		1							
Mar 26	Benjamin Wright	3										
Mar 26	Ellis Wright	1	1		1							
Mar 30	William Wright	1	1		2							
Apl 22	Moses Wright	1										
May 6	William B Wright	1										

Appendix: Amherst County, Virginia, 1847 Personal Property Tax List

Persons Chargeable With Tax [continued from prior page]	Metallic clocks	Other Clocks	Pianos and value	Plate over the value of $50	Attornies paying specific tax, and am't of tax	Physicians and surgeons paying specific tax, and amount of tax	Dentists paying specific tax, and amount of tax	Am't of int. of profits on moneys loaned out, or on bonds acquired by purchase, including interest, profits, or dividends, on state or corporat'n bonds	Am't of monied yearly income over $400 received as salaries or as fees of office
Henry T Wright	1								
Thomas Wright									
Lewis Wright									
Fielding H Wright									
Shelton H Wright									
Benjamin Wright									
Ellis Wright		1							
William Wright	1								
Moses Wright									
William B Wright		1							

Appendix: Amherst County, Virginia, 1847 Personal Property Tax List

Persons Chargeable With Tax [continued from prior page]	Bridges- am't of yearly rent or value over $100	Ferries- am't of yearly rent or value over $100	Newspaper printing presses and amount of tax	Total am't of tax Dollars Cents.	Identification
Henry T Wright				.80	1914 Henry Talley Wright of Amherst County, son of William Wright (Hanover County Tailor)
Thomas Wright				.96	
Lewis Wright				.20	1860 Lewis Wright of Lynchburg
Fielding H Wright				.32	Fielding Hobson Wright, son of 1873 Robert D. Wright of Amherst County, probably grandson of Charles Wright, and probably great grandson of Robert Wright, Sr. (Campbell County)
Shelton H Wright				.42	1862 Shelton H. Wright of Amherst County, son of 1873 Jesse Wright of Amherst County, grandson of 1830 Moses Wright of Amherst County, great grandson of 1799 Benjamin Wright of Amherst County, and great great grandson of 1767 Francis Wright of Amherst County
Benjamin Wright					Benjamin Wright, son of 1830 Moses Wright of Amherst County, grandson of 1799 Benjamin Wright of Amherst County, and great grandson of 1767 Francis Wright of Amherst County
Ellis Wright				.55	1880 Ellis Wright of Amherst County, son of 1850 Jesse Wright of Nelson County, grandson of 1799 Benjamin Wright of Amherst County, and great grandson of 1767 Francis Wright of Amherst County
William Wright				.77	1870 William Wright of Amherst County, son of 1850 Jesse Wright of Nelson County, grandson of 1799 Benjamin Wright of Amherst County, and great grandson of 1767 Francis Wright of Amherst County
Moses Wright					Probably 1849 Moses Wright of Nelson County, son of 1830 Moses Wright of Amherst County, grandson of 1799 Benjamin Wright of Amherst County, and great grandson of 1767 Francis Wright of Amherst County
William B Wright				.13	

1927(102507)

Appendix: Amherst County, Virginia, 1847 Personal Property Tax List

	Persons Chargeable With Tax	Whites above 16 years of age	Slaves above 15 years of age	Slaves above 12 years of age	Horses Mules &c	4 wheel pleasure carriages and harness and value	Stages, and value, including harness	Carryalls and harness, and value	2 wheel pleasure carriages and harness and Value	Gold watches	Patent lever or lapine silver watches	Other watches
May 8	William Wright	1	2	1	2							
May 15	Robert D Wright	1			1							
May 27	Benj. Wright jr	1			1							
May 27	Jesse Wright jr	1			1							

Appendix: Amherst County, Virginia, 1847 Personal Property Tax List

Persons Chargeable With Tax [continued from prior page]	Metallic clocks	Other Clocks	Pianos and value	Plate over the value of $50	Attornies paying specific tax, and am't of tax	Physicians and surgeons paying specific tax, and amount of tax	Dentists paying specific tax, and amount of tax	Am't of int. of profits on moneys loaned out, or on bonds acquired by purchase, including interest, profits, or dividends, on state or corporat'n bonds	Am't of monied yearly income over $400 received as salaries or as fees of office
William Wright	1								
Robert D Wright									
Benj. Wright jr									
Jesse Wright jr									

Appendix: Amherst County, Virginia, 1847 Personal Property Tax List

Persons Chargeable With Tax [continued from prior page]	Bridges- am't of yearly rent or value over $100	Ferries- am't of yearly rent or value over $100	Newspaper printing presses and amount of tax	Total am't of tax Dollars Cents.	Identification
William Wright				1.41	1851 William Wright of Amherst County, probably son of William Wright, Jr., and grandson of William Wright (Amherst County)
Robert D Wright				.10	1873 Robert D. Wright of Amherst County, probably son of Charles Wright and probably grandson of Robert Wright, Sr. (Campbell County)
Benj. Wright jr				.10	Benjamin Wright, son of Benjamin Wright, grandson of 1830 Moses Wright of Amherst County, great grandson of 1799 Benjamin Wright of Amherst County, and great great grandson of 1767 Francis Wright of Amherst County
Jesse Wright jr				.10	1873 Jesse Wright of Amherst County, son of 1830 Moses Wright of Amherst County, grandson of 1799 Benjamin Wright of Amherst County, and great grandson of 1767 Francis Wright of Amherst County

1848 PERSONAL PROPERTY TAX LIST

AMHERST COUNTY, VIRGINIA

Appendix: Amherst County, Virginia, 1848 Personal Property Tax List

	Persons Chargeable With Tax	Whites above 16 years of age	Slaves above 15 years of age	Slaves above 12 years of age	Horses Mules &c	4 wheel pleasure carriages and harness and value	Stages, and value, including harness	Carryalls and harness, and value	2 wheel pleasure carriages and harness and Value	Gold watches	Patent lever or lapine silver watches	Other watches
Feby 14	Lewis Wright	2			1							
Mar 20	William Wright	1	1		1							
Mar 25	Thomas Wright		2									
Apl 3	William B Wright	1										
Apl 8	Fielding H Wright	1	1									
May 10	Robert D Wright	2			1							
May 13	William Wright		2	1	2							
May 31	Shelton H Wright	1			1							
June 1	William Wright	1	1		2							
June 1	Ellis Wright	1	1		1							

Appendix: Amherst County, Virginia, 1848 Personal Property Tax List

Persons Chargeable With Tax [continued from prior page]	Metallic clocks	Other Clocks	Pianos and value	Plate over the value of $50	Attornies paying specific tax, and am't of tax	Physicians and surgeons paying specific tax, and amount of tax	Dentists paying specific tax, and amount of tax	Am't of int. of profits on moneys loaned out, or on bonds acquired by purchase, including interest, profits, or dividends, on state or corporat'n bonds	Am't of monied yearly income over $400 received as salaries or as fees of office
Lewis Wright									
William Wright		1							
Thomas Wright									
William B Wright		1							
Fielding H Wright									
Robert D Wright									
William Wright	1								
Shelton H Wright									
William Wright	1								
Ellis Wright	1								

1927(102507)

237.

Appendix: Amherst County, Virginia, 1848 Personal Property Tax List

Persons Chargeable With Tax [continued from prior page]	Bridges- am't of yearly rent or value over $100	Ferries- am't of yearly rent or value over $100	Newspaper printing presses and amount of tax	Total am't of tax Dollars Cents.	Identification
Lewis Wright					1860 Lewis Wright of Lynchburg
William Wright				.55	1870 William Wright of Amherst County, son of 1850 Jesse Wright of Nelson County, grandson of 1799 Benjamin Wright of Amherst County, and great grandson of 1767 Francis Wright of Amherst County [possible duplicate listing]
Thomas Wright				.10	
William B Wright				.13	
Fielding H Wright				.57	Fielding Hobson Wright, son of 1873 Robert D. Wright of Amherst County, probably grandson of Charles Wright, and probably great grandson of Robert Wright, Sr. (Campbell County)
Robert D Wright				.10	1873 Robert D. Wright of Amherst County, probably son of Charles Wright and probably grandson of Robert Wright, Sr. (Campbell County)
William Wright				1.41	1851 William Wright of Amherst County, probably son of William Wright, Jr., and grandson of William Wright (Amherst County)
Shelton H Wright				.10	1862 Shelton H. Wright of Amherst County, son of 1873 Jesse Wright of Amherst County, grandson of 1830 Moses Wright of Amherst County, great grandson of 1799 Benjamin Wright of Amherst County, and great great grandson of 1767 Francis Wright of Amherst County
William Wright				.77	1870 William Wright of Amherst County, son of 1850 Jesse Wright of Nelson County, grandson of 1799 Benjamin Wright of Amherst County, and great grandson of 1767 Francis Wright of Amherst County [possible duplicate listing]
Ellis Wright				.67	1880 Ellis Wright of Amherst County, son of 1850 Jesse Wright of Nelson County, grandson of 1799 Benjamin Wright of Amherst County, and great grandson of 1767 Francis Wright of Amherst County

1927(102507)

Appendix: Amherst County, Virginia, 1848 Personal Property Tax List

	Persons Chargeable With Tax	Whites above 16 years of age	Slaves above 15 years of age	Slaves above 12 years of age	Horses Mules &c	4 wheel pleasure carriages and harness and value	Stages, and value, including harness	Carryalls and harness, and value	2 wheel pleasure carriages and harness and Value	Gold watches	Patent lever or lapine silver watches	Other watches
June 4	Jesse Wright	1			1							
June 4	Henry T Wright	1	1									1

Appendix: Amherst County, Virginia, 1848 Personal Property Tax List

Persons Chargeable With Tax [continued from prior page]	Metallic clocks	Other Clocks	Pianos and value	Plate over the value of $50	Attornies paying specific tax, and am't of tax	Physicians and surgeons paying specific tax, and amount of tax	Dentists paying specific tax, and amount of tax	Am't of int. of profits on moneys loaned out, or on bonds acquired by purchase, including interest, profits, or dividends, on state or corporat'n bonds	Am't of monied yearly income over $400 received as salaries or as fees of office
Jesse Wright									
Henry T Wright	1								

Appendix: Amherst County, Virginia, 1848 Personal Property Tax List

Persons Chargeable With Tax [continued from prior page]	Bridges- am't of yearly rent or value over $100	Ferries- am't of yearly rent or value over $100	Newspaper printing presses and amount of tax	Total am't of tax Dollars Cents.	Identification
Jesse Wright				.10	1873 Jesse Wright of Amherst County, son of 1830 Moses Wright of Amherst County, grandson of 1799 Benjamin Wright of Amherst County, and great grandson of 1767 Francis Wright of Amherst County
Henry T Wright				.70	1914 Henry Talley Wright of Amherst County, son of William Wright (Hanover County Tailor)

1849 PERSONAL PROPERTY TAX LIST

AMHERST COUNTY, VIRGINIA

Appendix: Amherst County, Virginia, 1849 Personal Property Tax List

	Persons Chargeable With Tax	Whites above 16 years of age	Slaves above 15 years of age	Slaves above 12 years of age	Horses Mules &c	4 wheel pleasure carriages and harness and value	Stages, and value, including harness	Carryalls and harness, and value	2 wheel pleasure carriages and harness and Value	Gold watches	Patent lever or lapine silver watches	Other watches
Mar 17	Henry T Wright	1	1									1
Apl 9	Lewis Wright	2			1							
Apl 26	Shelton H Wright	1			1							
Apl 26	Jesse Wright	1			1							
Apl 26	William Wright	1	1		2							
Apl 26	Ellis Wright	1	1		1							
Apl 28	William Wright	2	1		2							
May 3	Robert D Wright	1			1							
May 3	David S Wright	1										

Appendix: Amherst County, Virginia, 1849 Personal Property Tax List

Persons Chargeable With Tax [continued from prior page]	Metallic clocks	Other Clocks	Pianos and value	Plate over the value of $50	Attornies paying specific tax, and am't of tax	Physicians and surgeons paying specific tax, and amount of tax	Dentists paying specific tax, and amount of tax	Am't of int. of profits on moneys loaned out, or on bonds acquired by purchase, including interest, profits, or dividends, on state or corporat'n bonds	Am't of monied yearly income over $400 received as salaries or as fees of office
Henry T Wright		1							
Lewis Wright									
Shelton H Wright									
Jesse Wright									
William Wright		1							
Ellis Wright									
William Wright	1								
Robert D Wright									
David S Wright									

Appendix: Amherst County, Virginia, 1849 Personal Property Tax List

Persons Chargeable With Tax [continued from prior page]	Bridges- am't of yearly rent or value over $100	Ferries- am't of yearly rent or value over $100	Newspaper printing presses and amount of tax	Total am't of tax Dollars Cents.	Identification
Henry T Wright				.70	1914 Henry Talley Wright of Amherst County, son of William Wright (Hanover County Tailor)
Lewis Wright				.10	1860 Lewis Wright of Lynchburg
Shelton H Wright				.10	1862 Shelton H. Wright of Amherst County, son of 1873 Jesse Wright of Amherst County, grandson of 1830 Moses Wright of Amherst County, great grandson of 1799 Benjamin Wright of Amherst County, and great great grandson of 1767 Francis Wright of Amherst County
Jesse Wright				.10	1873 Jesse Wright of Amherst County, son of 1830 Moses Wright of Amherst County, grandson of 1799 Benjamin Wright of Amherst County, and great grandson of 1767 Francis Wright of Amherst County
William Wright				.77	1870 William Wright of Amherst County, son of 1850 Jesse Wright of Nelson County, grandson of 1799 Benjamin Wright of Amherst County, and great grandson of 1767 Francis Wright of Amherst County
Ellis Wright				.42	1880 Ellis Wright of Amherst County, son of 1850 Jesse Wright of Nelson County, grandson of 1799 Benjamin Wright of Amherst County, and great grandson of 1767 Francis Wright of Amherst County
William Wright				1.41	1851 William Wright of Amherst County, probably son of William Wright, Jr., and grandson of William Wright (Amherst County)
Robert D Wright				.10	1873 Robert D. Wright of Amherst County, probably son of Charles Wright and probably grandson of Robert Wright, Sr. (Campbell County)
David S Wright					David Staples Wright, son of 1873 Robert D. Wright of Amherst County, probably grandson of Charles Wright, and probably great grandson of Robert Wright, Sr. (Campbell County)

1927(102507)

246.

Appendix: Amherst County, Virginia, 1849 Personal Property Tax List

Persons Chargeable With Tax	Whites above 16 years of age	Slaves above 15 years of age	Slaves above 12 years of age	Horses Mules &c	4 wheel pleasure carriages and harness and value	Stages, and value, including harness	Carryalls and harness, and value	2 wheel pleasure carriages and harness and Value	Gold watches	Patent lever or lapine silver watches	Other watches
May 29 Fielding H Wright	1										

Appendix: Amherst County, Virginia, 1849 Personal Property Tax List

Persons Chargeable With Tax [continued from prior page]	Metallic clocks	Other Clocks	Pianos and value	Plate over the value of $50	Attornies paying specific tax, and am't of tax	Physicians and surgeons paying specific tax, and amount of tax	Dentists paying specific tax, and amount of tax	Am't of int. of profits on moneys loaned out, or on bonds acquired by purchase, including interest, profits, or dividends, on state or corporat'n bonds	Am't of monied yearly income over $400 received as salaries or as fees of office
Fielding H Wright		1							

Appendix: Amherst County, Virginia, 1849 Personal Property Tax List

Persons Chargeable With Tax [continued from prior page]	Bridges- am't of yearly rent or value over $100	Ferries- am't of yearly rent or value over $100	Newspaper printing presses and amount of tax	Total am't of tax Dollars Cents.	Identification
Fielding H Wright				.25	Fielding Hobson Wright, son of 1873 Robert D. Wright of Amherst County, probably grandson of Charles Wright, and probably great grandson of Robert Wright, Sr. (Campbell County)

250.

1850 PERSONAL PROPERTY TAX LIST
AMHERST COUNTY, VIRGINIA

Appendix: Amherst County, Virginia, 1850 Personal Property Tax List

	Persons Chargeable With Tax	White Males above 16 years of age	Male free negroes above sixteen	Slaves above 16 years of age	Slaves above 12 years of age	Horses Mules &c	4 wheel pleasure carriages and harness and value	Stages, and value, including harness	Carryalls and harness, and value	2 wheel pleasure carriages and harness and value	Gold watches	Patent lever or lepine silver watches	Other watches
Feb 12	Lewis Wright	2				3							
Feb 12	James Wright	1											
Feb 12	Henry T Wright	1		1									1
Feb 12	William Wright			3		2							
Apl 5	Jesse Wright	1				1							
Apl 5	William Wright	1		1		1							
	Robert D Wright	1				1							
	Fielding H Wright	1		1									

Appendix: Amherst County, Virginia, 1850 Personal Property Tax List

Persons Chargeable With Tax [continued from prior page]	Metallic clocks	Other Clocks	Pianos and value	Harps and value	Plate over the value of $50	Attornies paying specific tax, and amount of tax	Physicians and surgeons paying specific tax, and amount of tax	Amount of interest or profits on moneys loaned out, or on bonds acquired by purchase, including interest, profits, or dividends, on state or corporation bonds	Amount of monied yearly income over $400 received as salaries or as fees of office
Lewis Wright									
James Wright									
Henry T Wright		1							
William Wright	1								
Jesse Wright									
William Wright	1								
Robert D Wright									
Fielding H Wright									

Appendix: Amherst County, Virginia, 1850 Personal Property Tax List

Persons Chargeable With Tax [continued from prior page]	Bridges- am't of yearly rent or value over $100	Ferries- am't of yearly rent or value over $100	Newspaper printing presses and amount of tax	Total amount of tax Dollars Cents.	Identification
Lewis Wright				.30	1860 Lewis Wright of Lynchburg
James Wright					
Henry T Wright				.70	1914 Henry Talley Wright of Amherst County, son of William Wright (Hanover County Tailor)
William Wright				1.41	1851 William Wright of Amherst County, probably son of William Wright, Jr., and grandson of William Wright (Amherst County)
Jesse Wright				.10	1873 Jesse Wright of Amherst County, son of 1830 Moses Wright of Amherst County, grandson of 1799 Benjamin Wright of Amherst County, and great grandson of 1767 Francis Wright of Amherst County
William Wright				.67	1870 William Wright of Amherst County, son of 1850 Jesse Wright of Nelson County, grandson of 1799 Benjamin Wright of Amherst County, and great grandson of 1767 Francis Wright of Amherst County
Robert D Wright				.10	1873 Robert D. Wright of Amherst County, probably son of Charles Wright and probably grandson of Robert Wright, Sr. (Campbell County)
Fielding H Wright				.32	Fielding Hobson Wright, son of 1873 Robert D. Wright of Amherst County, probably grandson of Charles Wright, and probably great grandson of Robert Wright, Sr. (Campbell County)

INDEX

Alfred, Mary, 176
Alfred, Susannah, 174
Edmunds, Samuel, 18, 19
Fitzgerald, Sam'l, 18, 19
Payne, Benjamin, 18, 19
Wright, Achilles, 64, 68, 73, 76, 84, 88
Wright, Achillis, 6, 80, 96
Wright, Achilus, 92
Wright, Ackillis, 18, 19
Wright, Alexander, 201, 215, 216, 217
Wright, Alexdr, 102
Wright, Allxr., 97
Wright, Ambrose F., 186
Wright, Andrew, 2, 6, 8, 12, 14, 18, 19, 22, 26, 30, 34, 38, 45, 48, 52, 56, 60, 64, 68, 72, 76, 81, 84, 88, 92, 96, 102
Wright, Archelus, 12
Wright, Archillis, 102
Wright, Augustin, 56, 60, 68, 73, 76
Wright, Augustine, 8, 12, 40
Wright, Austin, 92, 98, 103
Wright, Austuin, 80
Wright, Ben, 92
Wright, Benj, 97, 116, 103
Wright, jr., Benj., 231, 232, 233
Wright, Benjamain, 38
Wright, Benjamin, 2, 6, 8, 14, 20, 24, 26, 35, 44, 49, 53, 56, 60, 65, 69, 73, 77, 86, 90, 92, 104, 106, 108, 110, 112, 114, 122, 123, 124, 125, 129, 130, 133, 141, 149, 153, 156, 158, 164, 166, 168, 170, 174, 176, 178, 180, 182, 184, 186, 188, 191, 192, 196, 228, 229, 230
Wright, jr., Benjamin, 220, 221, 223
Wright, Jur., Benjamin, 215, 216, 217
Wright, Snr, Benjamin, 223, 224, 225
Wright, Benjn, 97, 103

Wright, Bennett, 94, 108
Wright, Burwell, 215, 216, 217
Wright, Cary, 156, 158, 160
Wright, Charles, 3, 178, 180, 182, 184, 186, 188, 192, 196
Wright, David, 40, 48, 53, 56, 60, 64, 68, 72
Wright, David S., 244, 245, 246
Wright, Ellis, 86, 90, 94, 188, 192, 196, 200, 208, 209, 210, 212, 213, 214, 220, 221, 222, 228, 229, 230, 236, 237, 238, 244, 245, 246
Wright, Fielding, 215, 216, 217, 222
Wright, Fielding H., 220, 221, 228, 229, 230, 236, 237, 238, 247, 248, 249, 252, 253, 254
Wright, Geo, 84, 88
Wright, George, 48, 53, 56, 57, 61, 64, 68, 81, 93, 96
Wright, Harrison, 161, 164, 168
Wright, Henry T., 208, 209, 210, 212, 213, 214, 220, 221, 222, 228, 229, 230, 239, 240, 241, 244, 245, 246, 252, 253, 254
Wright, Isaac, 2, 9, 14, 20, 24, 26, 28, 30, 32, 34, 36, 39, 41, 46, 48, 50, 57, 62, 66, 70, 74, 78, 82, 86, 90, 99, 104
Wright, jr., Isaac, 70, 74, 78, 82
Wright, Junr, Isaac, 86
Wright, Jur., Isaac, 90, 94, 99
Wright, Sen., Isaac, 94
Wright, James, 2, 6, 8, 12, 14, 18, 19, 22, 26, 30, 34, 35, 39, 44, 48, 52, 54, 56, 60, 61, 64, 68, 72, 73, 76, 81, 88, 93, 102, 103, 160, 164, 178, 180, 252, 253, 254
Wright, jr., James, 72, 76, 80
Wright, Senr., James, 73, 77, 80, 85, 102
Wright, Snr., James, 84
Wright, Sr., James, 22, 88
Wright, jr., Jas., 96

Wright, Senr., Jas, 96
Wright, Jesse, 20, 26, 30, 34, 35, 38, 44, 48, 49, 52, 96, 97, 103, 137, 142, 148, 153, 156, 158, 186, 196, 220, 221, 222, 239, 240, 241, 244, 245, 246, 252, 253, 254
Wright, jr., Jesse, 89, 96, 223, 224, 225, 231, 232, 233
Wright, Ju., Jesse, 129, 130, 178
Wright, Jun., Jesse, 170, 176
Wright, Junr., Jesse, 174, 182
Wright, Jur., Jesse, 133, 160, 164, 166, 168, 180, 184, 188, 190, 192, 200, 204, 205, 208, 209, 210, 212, 213, 214
Wright, Sr., Jesse, 88
Wright, Jesse K., 215, 216, 217
Wright, Jessee, 2, 8, 12, 14, 22, 27, 56, 64, 68, 72, 76, 77, 80, 88, 92
Wright, jr., Jessee, 60, 72, 84, 85
Wright, Senr., Jessee, 81
Wright, Jno., 18, 19, 97
Wright, John, 2, 6, 8, 12, 15, 18, 19, 22, 26, 30, 45, 48, 52, 56, 60, 64, 68, 72, 73, 76, 78, 80, 81, 82, 84, 88, 90, 92, 93, 94, 96, 99, 102, 104, 106, 108, 110, 114, 116, 122, 123, 124, 125, 129, 130, 133, 137, 141, 142, 148, 152, 156, 158, 160, 164, 168
Wright, Senr., John, 166
Wright, John W., 140
Wright, Jordan, 72, 76, 89
Wright, Jorden, 84, 85
Wright, Joseph, 174, 176, 178, 180, 182, 184, 186, 188, 191, 192, 201, 204, 205, 212, 213, 214
Wright, Kelles, 52
Wright, Killess, 48
Wright, Killis, 2, 8, 14, 22, 26, 31, 35, 39, 44

Wright, Landen, 85
Wright, Landon, 84, 89, 93
Wright, Lavina, 161, 164, 166, 170
Wright, Lewis, 158, 166, 168, 170, 174, 190, 204, 205, 212, 213, 214, 220, 221, 222, 228, 229, 230, 236, 237, 238, 244, 245, 246, 252, 253, 254
Wright, Lindsey, 76, 84, 85, 89, 92
Wright, Linsey, 68, 72
Wright, Linzey, 80
Wright, Mauris, 62, 66
Wright, Menos, 2, 6, 8, 14, 61, 64, 68, 72, 76
Wright, Menus, 26, 30, 34, 39, 44
Wright, Minos, 56
Wright, Minous, 96, 102
Wright, Mnos, 15
Wright, Moris, 110
Wright, Morrice, 116
Wright, Morris, 70, 74, 78, 114, 122, 123, 124, 125, 150
Wright, Morriss, 57, 82, 86, 90, 94, 99, 104, 129, 130, 133, 137, 141, 152, 156
Wright, Moses, 2, 3, 6, 8, 14, 20, 24, 32, 36, 74, 78, 82, 86, 90, 94, 99, 104, 106, 108, 112, 114, 116, 133, 137, 141, 160, 166, 288, 229, 230
Wright, Jr., Moses, 28, 110, 112, 116, 122, 123, 124, 125
Wright, Ju., Moses, 134, 148, 158, 152
Wright, Junr., Moses, 24, 114
Wright, Jur., Moses, 108, 129, 130, 137, 141
Wright, Sen., Moses, 152
Wright, Senr., Moses, 141, 148, 156
Wright, Snr., Moses, 129, 130
Wright, Sr., Moses, 110, 112, 122, 123, 124, 125
Wright, Mosses, 20
Wright, Parmenas, 48, 53
Wright, Parmenis, 84
Wright, Parmenus, 85, 92
Wright, Richard, 72, 76, 81, 168, 170, 172

Wright, Richard J., 160
Wright, Ro, 85
Wright, Robert, 2, 6, 8, 12, 14, 188, 19, 22, 26, 27, 30, 31, 34, 38, 44, 45, 49, 52, 56, 60, 64, 68, 72, 80, 84, 88, 96, 168, 220, 221, 222
Wright, Jr., Robert, 52
Wright (Senr), Robert, 48
Wright, Robert B., 178, 180
Wright, Robert D., 190, 197, 212, 213, 214, 231, 232, 233, 236, 237, 238, 244, 245, 246, 252, 253, 254
Wright, Robt, 73, 92, 97, 102
Wright, Rot, 102
Wright, Saml., 18
Wright, Samuel, 22, 36, 54, 66, 70, 74, 78, 82, 86
Wright, Shelton, 174, 182, 184, 196, 204, 205, 223, 224, 225
Wright, Jur., Shelton, 191
Wright, Shelton H., 200, 204, 205, 2113, 214, 208, 209, 210, 212, 228, 229, 230, 236, 237, 238, 244, 245, 246
Wright, Thomas, 6, 30, 53, 56, 61, 73, 76, 81, 148, 152, 156, 158, 208, 209, 210, 220, 221, 222, 228, 229, 230, 236, 237, 238
Wright, Thos, 128
Wright, Wiatt, 140
Wright, Wiett, 61
Wright, William, 2, 6, 8, 12, 14, 15, 18, 19, 34, 38, 40, 45, 48, 49, 52, 56, 60, 64, 65, 68, 72, 76, 80, 88, 92, 160, 164, 166, 168, 170, 172, 174, 176, 178, 180, 182, 184, 186, 188, 190, 192, 196, 197, 200, 201, 204, 205, 208, 209, 210, 212, 213, 214, 215, 216, 217, 220, 221, 222, 228, 229, 230, 231, 232, 233, 236, 237, 238, 244, 245, 246, 252, 253, 254
Wright, Jr., William, 22, 30
Wright, Jun., William, 26
Wright, Senr., William, 26

Wright, Sr., William, 23
Wright, William B., 196, 201, 220, 221, 222, 228, 229, 230, 236, 237, 238
Wright, William S., 200, 204, 205
Wright, Wm., 97, 118, 119, 120, 121, 102, 176

Other Heritage Books by Robert N. Grant

Identifying the Wrights in the Goochland County, Virginia Tithe Lists, 1732-84

The Identification of 1809 William Wright of Franklin County, Virginia, as the Son of 1792 John Wright of Fauquier County, Virginia, and Elizabeth (Bronaugh) (Darnall) Wright

Wright Family Birth Records (1853-1896) and Marriage Records (1788-1915): Franklin County, Virginia, 1853-1896

Wright Family Birth Records, 1853-1896; Marriage Records, 1761-1900; Census Records, 1810-1900 in Amherst County, Virginia

Wright Family Birth Records (1853-1896) and Marriage Records (1782-1900): Campbell County, Virginia

Wright Family Birth Records, Marriage Records, and Personal Property Tax Lists: Appomattox County, Virginia

Wright Family Census Records, Deed Records, Land Tax Lists, Death Records and Probate Records: Appomattox County, Virginia

Wright Family Census Records: Bedford County, Virginia, 1810-1900

Wright Family Census Records: Campbell County, Virginia, 1810-1900

Wright Family Census Records: Franklin County, Virginia, 1810-1900

Wright Family Death Records (1853-1920), Cemetery Records by Cemetery; and Probate Records (1782-1900): Campbell County, Virginia

Wright Family Death Records (1854-1920), Cemetery Records by Cemetery; and Probate Records (1785-1928): Franklin County, Virginia

Wright Family Death, Cemetery and Probate Records: Bedford County, Virginia

Wright Family Deed Records (1782-1900) and Land Tax List (1782-1850): Campbell County, Virginia

Wright Family Land Grants (1785-1900) and Deed Records (1785-1897): Franklin County, Virginia

Wright Family Land Grants, Deed Records, Land Tax List, Death Records, Probate Records: Prince Edward County, Virginia

Wright Family Land Tax Lists: Bedford County, Virginia

Wright Family Land Tax Lists: Franklin County, Virginia, 1786-1860

Wright Family Personal Property Tax Lists: Amherst County, Virginia, 1782-1850

Wright Family Personal Property Tax Lists: Campbell County, Virginia, 1785-1850

Wright Family Personal Property Tax Lists: Franklin County, Virginia, 1786-1850

Wright Family Personal Property Tax Records for Bedford County, Virginia, 1782 to 1850

Wright Family Records: Births in Bedford County, Virginia

Wright Family Records: Land Tax List, Bedford County, Virginia, 1782-1850

Wright Family Records: Lynchburg, Virginia Birth Records (1853-1896), Marriage Records (1805-1900), Marriage Notices (1794-1880), Census Records (1900), Deed Records (1805-1900), Death Records (1853-1896), Probate Records (1805-1900)

Wright Family Records: Marriages in Bedford County, Virginia

Wright Family Records: Prince Edward County, Virginia Birth Records, Marriage Records, Election Polls, and Tithe List, Personal Property Tax List, Census

www.ingramcontent.com/pod-product-compliance
Lightning Source LLC
Chambersburg PA
CBHW080429230426
43662CB00015B/2226